Barbs, Prongs, Points, Prickers, & Stickers

Barbs, Prongs, Points, Prickers, & Stickers

A Complete and Illustrated
Catalogue of Antique
Barbed Wire

Robert T. Clifton

University of Oklahoma Press

Standard Book Number: 8061–0876–2
(paper)
Standard Book Number: 8061–0875–4
(cloth)
Library of Congress Catalog Card Number: 78–88140

To my wife

Foreword

ALONG THE TRAIL of American history, there is an endless array of archival material and artifacts that attract and hold the interest of scholars and other people who look to the past for their pleasure as well as for information. When these objects of history lend themselves to grouping and can be moved, their accumulation becomes the goal of museums, libraries, and individuals. This collecting has become the hobby of an ever increasing number of American people who delight in gathering, exchanging, and hoarding "evidence" of a former time. The general trend is to concentrate on objects of inconsiderable size, such as buttons, bottles, spurs, bridle bits, and even fence wire.

The strong interest in antique barbed wire is indicated by the number of people who are actively discussing, collecting, trading, selling, and exhibiting it. So vigorous and impressive is the movement that people who, until recently, never knew there was more than one kind are making the various aspects of barbed wire the highlights of their conversation. Whenever farmers and ranchers gather to discuss crops, stock, and prices, stories of early barbed wire are likely to become part of the conversation. Displays can be seen in cafés, filling stations, and barbershops. Larger and more elaborate exhibits appear in museums and on the show boards of collectors.

Gripped with excitement, the collector searches farm and ranch lands for antique barbed wire. His hope is to find a "new" old wire. He may never find the elusive treasure, but he is found "looking out" ghost towns in New Mexico, checking faint remains of eastern Colorado homesteads, criss-crossing Kansas plains, or scouting lake shores and new expressway sites.

The men, women, and youngsters who engage in this hobby are scattered throughout the country. Among them are doctors, lawyers, engineers, teachers, students, and civil servants. They are determined that future generations will be able to view the evidence of the past which they have gathered with such patience and pleasure. Those "possessed" by this unusual hobby know the enjoyment it brings—an enjoyment that is equalled only by the curiosity of the uninformed, who observe and wonder what it is all about. For those who know what it is all about—who know the rewards of collecting a wire that had so important a role in the development of our country—this book is intended to serve as a helpful guide.

I regret that all who helped me cannot be listed, but I am deeply grateful to all of them. My greatest indebtedness, however, is to C. Boone McClure, Museum Director, and his staff, Panhandle-Plains Historical Museum, Canyon, Texas; Roscoe Rouse, Jr., University Librarian, and the Patents Section staff, Oklahoma State University, Stillwater, Oklahoma; and the personnel of the Correspondence and Mail Branch, United States Patent Office, Department of Commerce, Washington, D.C., for the co-operative and positive assistance provided when the material for the work was being collected.

I wish, also, to acknowledge indebtedness to the following collectors for their help and suggestions during the various stages of research and organization: Leo and Elva Shugart, Hoisington, Kansas; W. T. Swink, Olney, Texas; Hollis J. Gordon, Independence, Missouri; Watson W.

Davis, Greenwood, Missouri; William Crogan, Cheyenne, Wyoming; Lorena Ellicott, Van Tassell, Wyoming; Keith E. Hanna, Lexington, Nebraska; Tom Rawley, North Platte, Nebraska; Niels Miller, Herman, Nebraska; and Lawrence Long, Bowie, Texas.

And last, especial thanks are extended to Robert T. Clifton II, Denton, Texas; Leroy and Nancy Lutz, Henrietta, Texas; and Claude and Sarah Clifton, Flagstaff, Arizona, whose enthusiastic support and evaluation of the book in its early stages motivated and encouraged its completion.

ROBERT T. CLIFTON

July 1, 1969

Contents

SECTION III. BARS, RODS, WOODEN RAILS

SECTION IV. PICKETS

SECTION V. WARNING DEVICES

*A Complete and Illustrated
Catalogue of Antique
Barbed Wire*

They say that Heaven
*   is a free range land*
Good-by, Good-by, O fare you well;
But it's barbed wire fence
*   for the Devil's hat band*
And barbed wire blankets
*   down in Hell!*

—Old Cowboy Song

Introduction

THREE INVENTIONS are usually mentioned together as having exerted a profound influence in the settlement of the West: the revolver, the repeating rifle, and the windmill. During the past few years, however, it has been generally accepted that a fourth invention, that of barbed wire, wielded as great an influence and should be added to the list.

Like the other great inventions, barbed wire had the potential for serving man as soon as it came into existence. Made at a time when there was a pressing need for reliable fencing, by less than enthusiastic, experimenting farmers, almost overnight it developed into a source of wealth and furious litigation colored by impassioned charges and countercharges of patent infringement and greed.

The force that kept barbed fencing in existence, and kept the manufacturers from bogging down in the courts, was the continuing demand of Western homesteaders and ranchers for fencing that would shield them against outside dangers and protect their crops and livestock within.

In the mid-nineteenth century, the West was open range for the buffalo, mustang, longhorn, Indian, homesteader, and rancher. Each required something from the land that, in the taking, would jeopardize the security of the others.

To protect his small holdings, the homesteader fenced out the wild range animals and ranch stock. The rancher, in turn, was forced to fence range land, not only for grazing his cattle, but to establish claim to land that the sodbusters would surely take if he did not. Between the homesteader and the rancher, the buffalo, mustang, longhorn, and Indian were caught in an armored entanglement that brought them ever nearer to extermination.

The homesteader and the rancher, having little respect and consideration for each other, were often caught up in their own steel webs. Clashes were frequent and violent. Blood was shed by both sides. Good men died for putting fences up, and men equally good died for tearing fences down or cutting them.

In spite of the obstacles to its widespread use, barbed wire of every description was manufactured by legal and illegal means, and at great profit shipped west to fence the land. Hundreds of barbed-wire designs were invented. Although not all fencing was commercially successful, that which had practical value went by the carloads to the farms and ranches. There, where it was strung up so long ago, much of it still remains. This early barbed wire, however, is rapidly being replaced by modern wire with its lighter weight but higher tensile strength.

When old barbed wire is replaced, it is bypassed, left standing, or rolled up. That which is rolled up is piled in out-of-way corners of fields, hung in trees or on posts, thrown in junk heaps, or cast into rain-washed gullies to reduce soil erosion. The deserted fence rows and rolls of old wire are the sources of the antique barbed wire that is being searched out and carefully examined by collectors today. Perhaps the most difficult problem facing these wire collectors is "finding out" what they have found. There is a need for a well-organized system for identifying, classifying, and cataloging wire.

This book was developed to meet that need. Its organization was determined by the personal needs and interests of barbed-wire collectors and by the internal logic of a complex subject matter. The arrangement of the multitude of details offered no easy solution. In many instances, there initially seemed to be no clear ground for decision on classification; nevertheless, in sifting the material, the relationship of characteristics began to emerge and indicate the pattern that was adopted for classification.

The material readily separated itself into five sections: wire fencing; metallic strip fencing; bars, rods, and wooden rails; pickets; and warning devices. Of these, wire fencing and metallic strip fencing have been given primary consideration.

Wire fencing is divided into two subsections, barbless and barbed. The barbless wire is further subdivided by the number of strands, if plain wire; and by the design, if ornamental. Barbed wire is classified according to the number of strands, or as link wire, sectional wire, mesh wire, and interlaced fence strands. Each of these is further subdivided according to number of barb points. Finally, all items are grouped according to the barb design.

Metallic strip fencing is divided into four subsections: barbless strips, barb mounted strips, barb mounted double strips, and integrated barb strips. The barbless strips are divided further as flat, twist, corrugated, and sectional. Barb mounted strips and barb mounted double strips are divided, first according to number of barb points and, second, according to design. The integrated barb strips are divided according to design, and then according to the points, whether extended or extruded.

Since the identification of barbed wire and metallic strip fencing by style (gauge, length of barb, distance between barbs, coating, and so forth) is a subject that varies with the interest of each collector, only the basic designs of unidentified barbs, and basic designs and variations of patented barbs and barb strips are considered here. A patented item is indicated by a patent number enclosed in brackets. When the same number in brackets appears with additional items, it indicates that more than one design was submitted in the same patent. Variations of the patented items are identified by patent numbers without brackets.

Items in the last three sections of the book are identified in a manner similar to those in the first two sections. In the most part, they are fringe collectors' items and are included because of the interest factor rather than the value they give to a collection. Finally, all items are arranged in numerical order.

Three indexes are furnished the reader: one of patents, one of patentees, and another of by-names. These will be found valuable when used as references in conjunction with the detailed table of contents.

Some comments need to be made regarding by-names used in the book. Wherever possible, popular names are maintained; however, new names are used whenever the old conflicts with a general intent—that of making each one as totally descriptive of the item as practicable.

The bibliography reflects only the material used. Since reliance is placed heavily on patent data, the number of additional references is not extensive.

Section I. Wire Fencing

Wire fencing was especially adapted to use in the prairies and plains of the West, where stone was scarce, timber scanty, and hedges difficult to grow. It was simply designed, efficient, inexpensive, and of unlimited supply. It could be erected easily for either permanent or temporary and movable barriers. When broken, in disrepair, or damaged by the frequent fires that swept the grasslands, it could be mended or rebuilt from the wire that remained. It formed a passive barrier by pricking a warning to those animals seeking passage through it, but resisted with frightening effectiveness and cruelty those failing to turn away.

Wire fencing comprised any desired number of strands, smooth or barbed; however, because of the high tensile strength, one or two strands seemed strong enough for most needs. Yet it was light, flexible, and self-adjusting to expansion and contraction under changing temperature.

Wire fencing lent itself to an infinite variety of designs —exploited to the fullest by men who recognized the long-term benefits expectable from a good product. Hoping to profit as much as possible, the more ingenious inventors patented as many barbs as prior claims and their own creativeness permitted. Outstanding among these men were Edward M. Crandal, John D. Curtis, Thomas H. Dodge, William Edenborn, Franklin D. Ford, Joseph F. Glidden, J. Wool Griswold, Jacob Haish, Hiram B. Scutt, and Andrew J. Upham.

BARBLESS WIRE

Plain: *One Strand*

1   Plain One-strand Wire Fencing
Single-strand wire fencing. Wire is used alone, or alternately with barbed wire, in a fence.

2   Plain One-strand Wire Fencing
Single-strand wire fencing. Wire is used alone, or alternately with barbed wire, in a fence.

3   Plain One-strand Wire Fencing
Single-strand, soft-iron wire fencing. Wire is used alone, or alternately with barbed wire, in a fence.

Plain: *Two Strand*

4   Plain Two-strand Wire Fencing
Two-strand wire fencing. Twist prevents wire from breaking and sagging during expansion and contraction.

5   Plain Large–Small-strand Wire Fencing
Large–small-strand wire fencing. Wire is used alone, or alternately with barbed wire, in a fence.

Plain: *Three Strand*

Plain Three-strand Wire Fencing   6

Three-strand wire fencing. Fencing is used in place of two-strand wire where greater strength is needed.

Plain: *Half Round*

Plain Half-round Wire Fencing   7

Single-strand, half-round wire fencing. Twist in strand provides for expansion and contraction.

Plain: *Square*

Spiraling Square Wire   8

Spiraling square fence wire. Wire is used alone, or alternately with barbed wire, in a fence.

Plain: *Undulating*

Meriwether's Cold-weather Wire   9

Single-strand spiral undulating wire. Shape of wire allows for expansion and contraction. Patented [10211] November 8, 1853, by William H. Meriwether of New Braunfels, Tex.

Ornamental: *Braid*

10 Preston's Braid
Three-strand wire braid. Patented [248348] October 18, 1881,
by Othniel Preston of Hornellsville, N.Y.

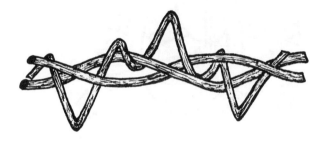

11 Reynolds' Web
Two-strand ornamental fence wire with interlocking third
wire composed of a series of bends and projections. Patented
[287391] October 23, 1883, by William R. Reynolds of
Rahway, N.J.

12 Brock's Take-up Knot
Single-strand wire in an ornamental take-up knot design.
Patented [293412] February 12, 1884, by William E. Brock
of New York, N.Y.

Grosvenor's Loop and Bend Ornamental Fencing   13

Three-strand interlacing ornamental wire fencing. One strand formed of bends anchors to twisted double strands. Patented [453272] June 2, 1891, by George H. Grosvenor of Hornellsville, N.Y.

Shellaberger's Loops   14

Four-strand interlaced ornamental wire fencing. Patented [465391] December 15, 1891, by M. M. Shellaberger of Beaver Falls, Pa.

Shellaberger's Spaced Loops   15

Four-strand interlaced ornamental wire fencing. Patented [465391] December 15, 1891, by M. M. Shellaberger of Beaver Falls, Pa.

Shellaberger's Zigzag   16

Three-strand interlaced ornamental wire fencing. Patented [465391] December 15, 1891, by M. M. Shellaberger of Beaver Falls, Pa.

17 Shellaberger's Long Zigzag
Three-strand interlaced ornamental wire fencing. Patented [465391] December 15, 1891, by M. M. Shellaberger of Beaver Falls, Pa.

18 Shellaberger's Snake Wrap
Two-strand ornamental wire fencing. Patented [465391] December 15, 1891, by M. M. Shellaberger of Beaver Falls, Pa.

19 Cleaveland's Weave and Twist
Four-strand ornamental wire consisting of two weaving and two twisting strands. Patented [486824] November 22, 1892, by John B. Cleaveland of Indianapolis, Ind.

20 Riter's Corrugated Visible Wire
Three-strand braided corrugated fencing. Patented [506257] October 10, 1893, by John L. Riter of Brownsville, Ind.

Cleaveland's Weave   21

Four-strand interwoven wire fencing. Paired strands do not cross. Patented [516886] March 20, 1894, by John B. Cleaveland of Indianapolis, Ind.

Wright's Ornamental Wire   22

Four-strand ornamental wire with inside twisting strands and outside spiraling parallel strands. Patented [517256] March 27, 1894, by George C. Wright of Indianapolis, Ind.

Cleaveland's Spiral Twist   23

Four-strand visible wire fencing. Fencing consists of twisted double strands. Doubled strands twist around each other. Patented [522826] July 10, 1894, by John B. Cleaveland of Indianapolis, Ind.

Ornamental: *Panel*

24 Walking Wire
Two parallel wire strands joined by interlocking cross wire.
Inventor of wire is unknown.

25 Loop and Hitch Ornamental Fencing
Two parallel looping-edge strands binding loops in a cross
wire. Inventor of wire is unknown.

26 Miles' Barbless Parallel
Two parallel wire strands joined with zigzagging cross wire.
Patented [277917] May 22, 1883, by Purches Miles of Brook-
lyn, N.Y.

Miles' Barbless Parallel, Wide Variation   27
Two parallel wire strands joined by interlacing cross wire.
Variation of patent 277917.

Miles' Barbless Parallel, Three-strand Variation   28
Three parallel wire strands joined by interlacing cross wires.
Variation of patent 277917.

Hathaway–Woodard's Center Twist Ornamental Wire   29
Six-strand interlacing ornamental wire. Parallel double strands
run through the center. Patented [433940] August 12, 1890,
by William E. Hathaway and Alonzo B. Woodard of Hor-
rellsville, N.Y.

30 Hathaway–Woodard's Center Weave Ornamental Wire
Six-strand interlacing ornamental wire. Parallel double strands weave through the center. Patented [433940] August 12, 1890, by William E. Hathaway and Alonzo B. Woodard of Hornellsville, N.Y.

31 Hathaway–Woodard's Ornamental Wire, Edge Weave Variation
Six-strand interlacing ornamental wire. Parallel double strands weave down the edges. Variation of patent 433940.

32 Hathaway–Woodard's Ornamental Wire, Twist-edge Variation
Six-strand interlacing ornamental wire. Parallel twisted strands run along the edges. Variation of patent 433940.

Woodard's Ornamental Loops   33

Four-strand intertwining ornamental wire. Loops wrap
around twisted double strand down the center. Patented
[447927] March 10, 1891, by Alonzo B. Woodard of Hornellsville, N.Y.

Ingraham's Visible Loop Wire Fencing   34

Four-strand visible wire fencing. Double twisted strands loop
and tie at intervals. Patented [469062] February 16, 1892, by
T. J. Ingraham of Hornellsville, N.Y.

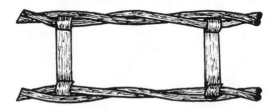

Curtis' Ladder   35

Parallel twisted two-strand wire joined by sheet metal straps.
Patented [494551] April 4, 1893, by John D. Curtis of Worcester, Mass.

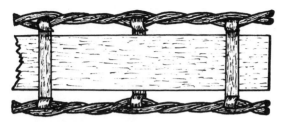

36 Curtis' Ladder with Slat
Parallel twisted two-strand wire joined by sheet metal straps.
Sheet metal strip is inserted between straps for greater visibility. Patented [494551] April 4, 1893, by John D. Curtis of
Worcester, Mass.

37 Riter's Visible Lace Wire
Parallel undulating single-wire strands joined by intertwining
smaller wire. Patented [506258] October 10, 1893, by John L.
Riter of Brownsville, Ind.

Ornamental: *Loop*

38 Cleaveland's Half-loop Visible Wire Fencing
Single-strand wire with ornamental wire loops. Patented
[475718] May 24, 1892, by John B. Cleaveland of Indianapolis,
Ind.

Cleaveland's Full-loop Visible Wire Fencing   39

Single-strand wire with ornamental wire coils. Patented
[475718] May 24, 1892, by John B. Cleaveland of Indianapolis,
Ind.

Cleaveland's Undulating Visible Wire Fencing   40

Two-strand undulating ornamental wire. Outer strand loops
and wraps around central undulating strand. Patented
[475719] May 24, 1892, by John B. Cleaveland of Indianapolis,
Ind.

Cleaveland's Zigzag Visible Wire Fencing   41

Two-strand ornamental wire fencing. Outer strand loops and
wraps around central zigzag strand. Patented [475719] May
24, 1892, by John B. Cleaveland of Indianapolis, Ind.

42

McNelly's Wide Loop

Single-strand wire with wire loop. Folds in loop extend in

opposite directions. Patented [539390] May 14, 1895, by
Mathias F. McNelly of Sterling, Ill.

43 McNelly's Single Loops

Single-strand wire with individual projecting loops. Ends of
one loop wrap in same direction around strand. Ends of the
other loop wrap around the strand in opposite direction.
Patented [539390] May 14, 1895, by Mathias F. McNelly of
Sterling, Ill.

44 McNelly's Pull-through Loop

Single-strand wire with projecting loops formed from wire
ring. Patented [539390] May 14, 1895, by Mathias F. McNelly
of Sterling, Ill.

45 Smith's Rings

Two-strand wire with opposed, visible circular projections.
Patented [578032] March 2, 1897, by Datus C. Smith of
Yonkers, N.Y.

Ornamental: *Spread*

Riter's Visible Wire   46

Two-strand fencing with alternating sections of loose and
tight twists. Patented [506256] October 10, 1893, by John L.
Riter of Brownsville, Ind.

Smith's Zigzag Spread   47

Two-strand wire with visible zigzag spreads. Patented
[578032] March 2, 1897, by Datus C. Smith of Yonkers, N.Y.

Smith's Spread Zigzag and Arch   48

Two-strand wire with visible zigzag and arched open spreads.
Patented [578032] March 2, 1897, by Datus C. Smith of
Yonkers, N.Y.

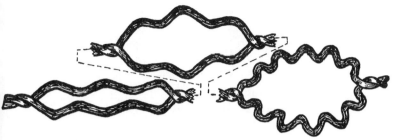

49 Smith's Spread Zigzag, Arch, and Leaf
Two-strand wire with visible zigzag, arched, and leaf-shaped spreads. Patented [578032] March 2, 1897, by Datus C. Smith of Yonkers, N.Y.

50 Smith's Wave Spread
Two-strand wire with visible undulating spread. Patented [578032] March 2, 1897, by Datus C. Smith of Yonkers, N.Y.

51 Smith's Arch
Two-strand wire with visible arched spread. Patented [578032] March 2, 1897, by Datus C. Smith of Yonkers, N.Y.

Smith's Square   52

Two-strand wire with visible square spread. Patented
[578032] March 2, 1897, by Datus C. Smith of Yonkers, N.Y.

Smith's Descending Beads   53

Two-strand wire with visible descending spreads. Patented
[578032] March 2, 1897, by Datus C. Smith of Yonkers, N.Y.

Smith's Oval, Double Variation   54

Two-strand visible wire. Variation of patent 578032.

BARBED WIRE: SINGLE STRAND

One-point Wire Barbs: *Loop*

55 Miles' Knife-edge
Single-strand wire looped and twisted at regular intervals. Loops are flattened to form knife-edge barbs. Patented [277916] May 22, 1883, by Purches Miles of Brooklyn, N.Y.

56 Miles' Open Diamond Point, One Strand
Single-strand wire looped and twisted at regular intervals. Loops are flattened and shaped to form barbs. Patented [277916] May 22, 1883, by Purches Miles of Brooklyn, N.Y.

57 Miles' Open Diamond Point, Double Strand
Two-strand wire with one strand looped and twisted at regular intervals. Loops are flattened and shaped to form barbs. Patented [277916] May 22, 1883, by Purches Miles of Brooklyn, N.Y.

25

Miles' Closed Diamond Point 58

Single-strand wire looped and twisted at regular intervals. Loops are flattened and shaped to form barbs. Patented [277916] May 22, 1883, by Purches Miles of Brooklyn, N.Y.

Miles' Pitted Point 59

Single-strand wire looped and twisted at regular intervals. Loops are flattened and cut to form barbs. Patented [277916] May 22, 1883, by Purches Miles of Brooklyn, N.Y.

One-point Wire Barbs: *Nail*

Horseshoe-nail Barb 60

Single-strand wire with horseshoe-nail barb. Barb is held in place by small-gauge wire spiral-wrapped around the wire strand. Fencing is hand assembled.

Two-point Wire Barbs: *Single Turn*

61 Big John
Single-strand wire with two-point wire barb. Barb is hand mounted. Inventor of barb is unknown.

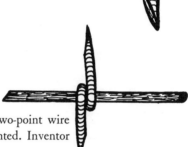

62 Long Tom
Single-strand wire with two-point wire barb. Barb is hand mounted. Inventor of barb is unknown.

63 Great Taper Barb
Single-strand wire with two-point, tapered-wire barb. Barb is held in position by a flattened inner surface. Inventor of barb is unknown.

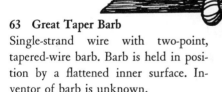

**64
Stover's
Single-wrap
Barb**

Single-strand wire with two-point wire barb. Barb points line up across the center of the coil. Patented [190167] May 1, 1877, by Daniel C. Stover of Freeport, Ill.

Dobbs' Grooved Fence Wire   65

Fence wire with spiraling grooves at intervals to receive and hold barbs in place. Patented [190836] May 15, 1877, by John Dobbs of Victor, Iowa.

Miles' Staple Barb   66

Single-strand wire with two-point wire barb made from fencing staple. Barb is hand mounted. Patented [208688] October 8, 1878, by Purches Miles of New York, N.Y.

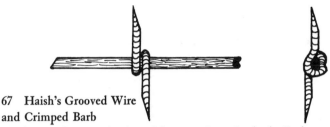

67   Haish's Grooved Wire and Crimped Barb

Single-strand grooved wire with two-point wire barb. Barb is crimped over groove in strand. Patented [261703] July 25, 1882, by Jacob Haish of De Kalb, Ill.

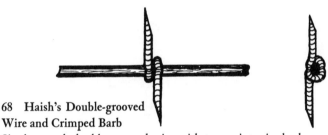

68   Haish's Double-grooved Wire and Crimped Barb

Single-strand, double-grooved wire with two-point wire barb. Barb is crimped over grooves in strand. Patented [261703] July 25, 1882, by Jacob Haish of De Kalb, Ill.

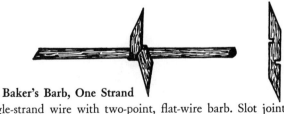

69   Baker's Barb, One Strand

Single-strand wire with two-point, flat-wire barb. Slot joint holds barb in place. Patented [273219] February 27, 1883, by George C. Baker of Des Moines, Iowa.

Brock's Barbed Take-up Knot   70

Single-strand wire in an ornamental take-up knot design with two-point wire barb. Patented [293412] February 12, 1884, by William E. Brock of New York, N.Y.

Two-point Wire Barbs: *Coil*

Hanging Barb, Square Strand   71

Single-strand, spiraling square wire with two-point wire barb. Points of barb extend in the same direction. Inventor of barb is unknown.

Glidden's Coil, Hanging-barb One-strand Variation   72

Single-strand wire with two-point wire barb. Variation of reissue patent 6913.

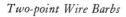

73 Glidden's Coils, Flattened-strand Variation

Flattened single-wire strand with two-point wire barb. Variation of reissue patent 6913.

74 Glidden's Barb, One-strand Variation

Single-strand wire with two-point wire barb. Variation of patent 157124.

75 Decker's Ribbed Fence Wire with Wire Barb

Single-strand ribbed fence wire showing non-slip advantage of wire barbs pressed into the rib. Patented [178605] June 13, 1876, by Alexander C. Decker of Bushnell, Ill.

76 Glidden's Twist Oval

Single-strand, oval-shaped wire with round wire barb. Shape of wire keeps barb from turning. Patented [181433] August 22, 1876, by Joseph F. Glidden of De Kalb, Ill.

77

**Glidden's Twist Oval,
Light Duty Variation**

Single-strand, oval-shaped wire with round wire barb. Variation of patent 181433.

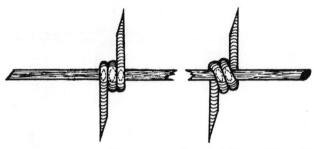

Putnam's Fence Wire   78

Fence wire with barbs pressed into the strand. Patented [187172] February 6, 1877, by Henry W. Putnam of Bennington, Vt.

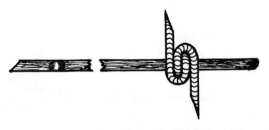

Upham's Coil, Round Strand   79

Single-strand wire with two-point wire barb. Indentation in strand prevents barb slipping. Patented [284261] September 4, 1883, by Andrew J. Upham of Sycamore, Ill.

**80 Upham's Coil,
Half-round Strand**
Twisted half-round wire strand with
two-point wire barb. Flat surface of
strand prevents barb turning. Patented
[284261] September 4, 1883, by Andrew J. Upham of Sycamore, Ill.

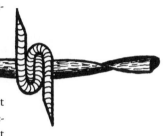

**81 Upham's Coil,
Twist-oval Strand Variation**
Twisted oval wire strand with two-point
wire barb. Oval surface of strand prevents barb turning. Variation of patent
284261.

**82 Lenox's
Single-knob Fence Wire**
Single-strand wire with two-point wire
barb. Barb is held in place by projection
on surface of strand. Patented [300783]
June 24, 1884, by Edwin S. Lenox of
Worcester, Mass.

**83 Haish's Wide-space
Ribbed Barb, Corrugated Wire**
Single-strand corrugated wire with two-
point, half-round wire barb. Barb is wide
wrapped and held in position by teeth
in flat surface. Patented [356762] February 1, 1887, by Jacob Haish of
De Kalb, Ill.

Haish's Wide-space Barb, Smooth Wire   84

Single-strand wire with two-point, half-round wire barb. Barb is wide wrapped and held in position by teeth in flat surface. Patented [356762] February 1, 1887, by Jacob Haish of De Kalb, Ill.

Rogers' Wire with Coil Barb   85

Single-strand wire with two-point wire barb. Wire strand is flattened and twisted between barbs. Patented [376418] January 10, 1888, by Charles D. Rogers of Providence, R.I.

86
Rogers' Non-slip Barb, Straight-strand Variation

Single-strand wire with two-point wire barb. Wire strand is flattened slightly between the barbs. Variation of patent 376418.

Two-point Wire Barbs: *Wrap*

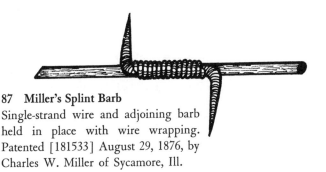

87   Miller's Splint Barb
Single-strand wire and adjoining barb
held in place with wire wrapping.
Patented [181533] August 29, 1876, by
Charles W. Miller of Sycamore, Ill.

88
Rose's Wide-wrap Barb
Single-strand, eight-sided wire with two-point, wide-wrap
barb. Patented [198688] December 25, 1877, by Henry M.
Rose of Waterman Station, Ill.

89   Rose's Wide-wrap Barb, One-strand Variation
Single-strand wire with two-point wire barb. Variation of
patent 198688.

Doerr's Electric Fence Wire   90

Single-strand wire with two-point wire barb. Wide wrapped barb and strand are pressed together. Patented [2909360] October 20, 1959, by Raymond S. Doerr of Battle Creek, Mich.

91
Smith's Edge-drilled Warning Block
and Two-point Barb

Single-strand wire with two-point wire barb and warning block. Barb passes through drilled hole in block and around wire strand. Patented [266545] October 24, 1882, by Eldridge J. Smith of Williamsport, Pa.

Smith's Side-drilled Warning Block   92
and Two-point Barb

Single-strand wire with two-point wire barb and warning block. Barb passes through drilled holes in block and around wire strand. Patented [266545] October 24, 1882, by Eldridge J. Smith of Williamsport, Pa.

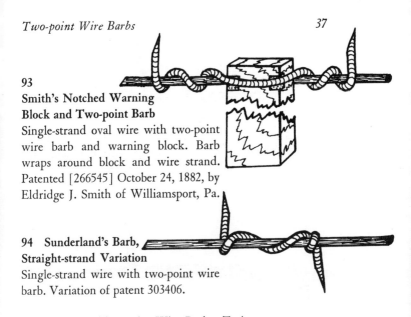

93
Smith's Notched Warning
Block and Two-point Barb
Single-strand oval wire with two-point
wire barb and warning block. Barb
wraps around block and wire strand.
Patented [266545] October 24, 1882, by
Eldridge J. Smith of Williamsport, Pa.

94 Sunderland's Barb,
Straight-strand Variation
Single-strand wire with two-point wire
barb. Variation of patent 303406.

Two-point Wire Barbs: *Twist*

95 Twist and Cut Barb
Twisted two-strand wire with one strand cut to form two-
point barbs. Inventor of barb is unknown.

96 Cut and Span Barb
Twisted two-strand wire with one strand cut to form two-
point spanner barbs. Inventor of barb is unknown.

Mack's Twist 97

Single-strand wire with two-point wire barb. Barb and wire twist together. Patented [162835] May 4, 1875, by Martin M. Mack of Boone, Ill.

Mighell's Winding Barb, One Strand 98

Single-strand wire with two-point, long-winding barbs. Patented [199924] February 5, 1878, by Montraville P. Mighell of Delta, Iowa.

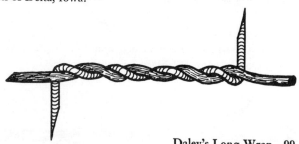

Daley's Long Wrap 99

Single-strand wire corrugated at intervals to accommodate winding two-point wire barbs. Patented [209467] October 29, 1878, by Michael Daley of Waterman, Ill.

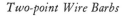

100 Daley's Caduceus
Single-strand wire corrugated at intervals to accommodate laced-on, two-point wire barbs. Patented [209467] October 29, 1878, by Michael Daley of Waterman, Ill.

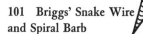

101 Briggs' Snake Wire and Spiral Barb
Single-strand spiraling undulating wire with two-point barb. Curves in wire keep the barb from slipping. Patented [301086] July 1, 1884, by Orlando P. Briggs of Chicago, Ill.

Two-point Wire Barbs: *Kink Locked*

102 Dobbs–Booth's Non-slip Staple Barb
Single-strand wire with two-point wire barb. Strand is kinked to hold barb in place. Patented [171105] December 14, 1875, by John Dobbs and Benjamin F. Booth of Victor, Iowa.

Emerson's Loop   103

Single-strand kinked wire with two-point wire barb. Barb is looped around strand and held in place by kink. Patented [176523] April 25, 1876, by Richard Emerson of Sycamore, Ill.

Sunderland's Kink   104

Single-strand wire with two-point wire barb. Strand is kinked to hold barbs in place. Patented [303406] August 12, 1884, by Leslie E. Sunderland of Joliet, Ill.

Sunderland's Kink,   105
Long Variation

Single-strand wire with two-point wire barb. Strand is kinked to hold barbs in place. Variation of patent 303406.

Sunderland's Kink,   106
Slant-strand Variation

Single-strand wire with two-point wire barb. Barb is locked around bend in strand. Variation of patent 303406.

107 Sunderland's Kink, Winding-barb Variation
Single-strand wire with two-point wire barb. Variation of patent 303406.

108 Woodruff–Hutchins' Kink
Single-strand wire with two-point wire barb. Kink in strand holds barb in place. Patented [308451] November 25, 1884, by Charles E. Woodruff and William J. Hutchins of Joliet, Ill.

109 Ford's Kink and Coil
Single-strand wire with two-point wire barb. Strand is kinked at intervals to receive coiled barbs. Patented [311426] January 27, 1885, by Franklin D. Ford of Providence, R.I.

Ford's Kink and Coil, 110
Modified-coil Variation
Single-strand wire with two-point wire
barb. Variation of patent 311426.

Ford's Kink and Twist, 111
One Strand
Single-strand wire with two-point wire
barb. Strand is kinked to receive twisted
barb. Patented [311740] February 3,
1885, by Franklin D. Ford of Providence, R.I.

Ford's Kink and Wrap Barb 112
Single-strand wire with two-point wire
barb. Strand is bent at intervals to hold
barbs in place. Patented [312454] February 17, 1885, by Franklin D. Ford of
Providence, R.I.

113 Hunt's Arch
Single-strand wire with two-point wire barb. Barb wraps around and locks in a loop in the strand. Patented [338229] March 16, 1886, by James E. Hunt of Chicago, Ill.

114 Kraft's Crimp, One Strand
Single-strand wire with two-point wire barb. Barb and strand are crimped to hold barb in place. Patented [341921] May 18, 1886, by Charles J. F. Kraft and Augustus C. H. Kraft of Joliet, Ill.

Two-point Wire Barbs: *Loop Locked*

115 Page's Half Hitch and Loop

Single-strand wire with two-point wire barb. Half hitch in strand holds barb in place. Patented [170891] December 7, 1875, by Justin E. Page of Sycamore, Ill.

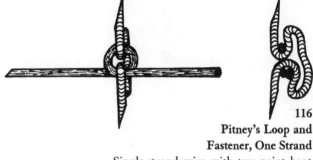

116
Pitney's Loop and
Fastener, One Strand
Single-strand wire with two-point bent
wire barb. Strand loops around barb to
hold it in position. Patented [208538]
October 1, 1878, by Albert L. Pitney of
Washington, D.C.

Schmeiser's Prongs   117
Single-strand wire with two-point barb
formed from the strand. Patented
[253632] February 14, 1882, by Henry
J. Schmeiser of Burlington, Iowa.

118
Locke's Loop Lock and Twist
Single-strand wire with two-point wire
barb. Barb passes through loop and
wraps around strand. Patented [277423]
May 8, 1883, by Charles S. Locke of
Joliet, Ill.

119 Stevens' Loop Lock
Single-strand wire with two-point wire barb. Patented
[291420] June 1, 1884, by Amasa W. Stevens of East Brook-
field, Mass.

120 Kelly's Swinging Barb, One Strand
Single-strand wire with two-point wire barb. Barb hangs
from loop in the strand. Patented [322108] July 14, 1885, by
Michael Kelly of New York, N.Y.

121 Kelly's Swinging Barb, Twist Loop
Single-strand wire with two-point wire barb. Barb hangs
from an eye twisted in the strand. Patented [322108] July 14,
1885, by Michael Kelly of New York, N.Y.

Two-point Wire Barbs: *Washer Locked*

122
Vosburgh's Washer-locked Barb, One Strand

Single-strand wire with two-point wire barb. Arched barb is locked in place on the strand with a slotted metal plate. Patented [182778] October 3, 1876, by Cyrus A. Vosburgh of Chicago, Ill.

123
Brunner–Reynolds' Two Point

Single-strand wire with staple barb and die-cut washer. Patented [200125] February 12, 1878, by Charles Brunner of Peru, and Hiram Reynolds of La Salle, Ill.

Dodge's Bent Wire and Ring   124

Single-strand wire with two-point, ring-locked barb. Patented [201507] March 19, 1878, by Thomas H. Dodge of Worcester, Mass.

Dodge's Ring-locked Barb   125

Single-strand wire with two-point wire barb flattened in the middle. Patented [201507] March 19, 1878, by Thomas H. Dodge of Worcester, Mass.

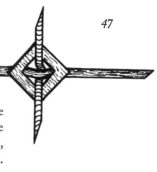

126 Case's Washer-locked Barb

Single-strand kinked wire with wire barb. Barb is locked in place with square washer. Patented [256880] April 25, 1882, by George Case of De Kalb, Ill.

Two-point Wire Barbs: *Clip*

127 Devore's Clip

Single-strand wire with two-point, looped-wire barb. Barb is crimped to the strand. Patented [168886] October 19, 1875, by Levi M. Devore of Yellow Creek, Ill.

128 Devore's Wire Lock

Single-strand wire with two-point, looped-wire barb. Barb is secured with wire lock. Patented [168886] October 19, 1875, by Levi M. Devore of Yellow Creek, Ill.

129 Nelson's Clip-on

Single-strand wire with two-point wire barb. Barbs are crimped to the strand. Patented [185346] December 12, 1876, by John Nelson of Creston, Ill.

Two-point Wire Barbs: *Hitch*

Wire Hitch   130

Single-strand wire with two-point wire barb. Multiple wraps
hold the barb in place. Inventor of barb is unknown.

Kittleson's Half Hitch   131

Single-strand wire with two-point wire barb. Barb is tied in
the form of a half hitch. Patented [189047] April 3, 1887, by
Ole O. Kittleson of Milan, Ill.

Two-point Wire Barbs: *Welded*

Perry's Cross Stick, One Strand   132

Single-strand wire with two-point wire barb. Barb is electrically welded to strand. Patented [588774] August 24, 1897,
by John C. Perry of Joliet, Ill.

133 Perry's Welded Barb, One Strand

Single-strand wire with two-point wire barb. Barb is electrically welded to strand. Patented [588774] August 24, 1897, by John C. Perry of Joliet, Ill.

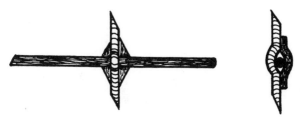

134 Perry's Saddle Barb, One Strand

Single-strand wire with wire and plate barb. Barb and plate are mounted on strand and electrically welded. Patented [588774] August 24, 1897, by John C. Perry of Joliet, Ill.

Three-point Barbs: *Clip and Nail*

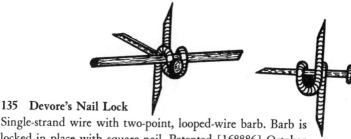

135 Devore's Nail Lock

Single-strand wire with two-point, looped-wire barb. Barb is locked in place with square nail. Patented [168886] October 19, 1875, by Levi M. Devore of Yellow Creek, Ill.

Three-point Barbs: *Wire and Barbed Washer*

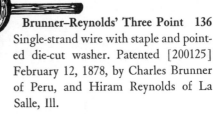

Brunner–Reynolds' Three Point   136
Single-strand wire with staple and pointed die-cut washer. Patented [200125] February 12, 1878, by Charles Brunner of Peru, and Hiram Reynolds of La Salle, Ill.

Four-point Wire Barbs: *Coil*

Modern Corrugated Wire   137
Single-strand corrugated wire with four-point wire barb. Bend in strand holds barb in place.

Glidden's Coils   138
Single-strand wire with four-point wire barb. Reissue patent [6914] February 8, 1876, by Joseph F. Glidden of De Kalb, Ill.

139   Glidden's Coils, Channeled Square-wire Variation
Single-strand square wire with four-point wire barb. One side of the strand is channeled. Variation of reissue patent 6914.

140   Glidden's Coils, Flute-rib Strand Variation
Single-strand wire with four-point wire barb. Strand is both fluted and ribbed. Variation of reissue patent 6914.

141   Glidden's Coils, Stretched Variation
Single-strand wire with four-point wire barb. Variation of reissue patent 6914.

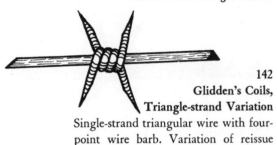

142
Glidden's Coils,
Triangle-strand Variation
Single-strand triangular wire with four-
point wire barb. Variation of reissue
patent 6914.

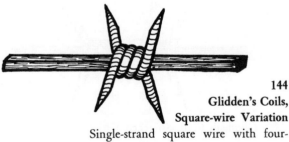

143
Glidden's Coils,
Spiraling-rib Strand Variation
Single-strand ribbed wire with four-
point wire barb. Coils are pressed into
the rib to hold barb in position. Variation of reissue patent 6914.

144
Glidden's Coils,
Square-wire Variation
Single-strand square wire with four-
point wire barb. Variation of reissue
patent 6914.

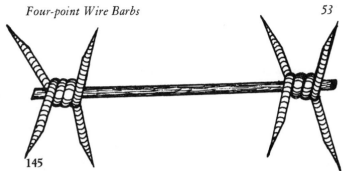

145

Glidden's Coils, One-strand Military Concertina Variation
One-strand high tensile strength wire with four-point wire barbs. Variation of patent reissue 6914.

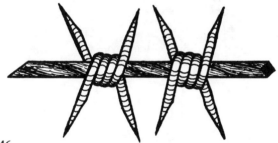

146

Glidden's Coils, Military Entanglement-wire Variation
Single-strand square wire with four-point wire barbs. Barbs are closely spaced along the strand. Variation of reissue patent 6914.

147 Merrill's Brads
Single-strand wire with four-point wire barb. Body of barb is tightly coiled to hold barb in position. Patented [155538] September 29, 1874, by Luther and John C. Merrill of Turkey River Station, Iowa.

Merrill's Four-point Coil 148

Single-strand wire with four-point wire barb. Pattern of barb changes as wire is turned. Patented [185688] December 26, 1876, by John C. Merrill of Turkey River Station, Iowa.

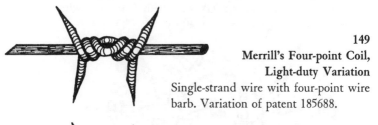

149
Merrill's Four-point Coil,
Light-duty Variation
Single-strand wire with four-point wire barb. Variation of patent 185688.

150
Lenox's Dual-knob Fence Wire
Single-strand wire with four-point wire barb. Barb is held in place by projections on surface of strand. Patented [300783] June 24, 1884, by Edwin S. Lenox of Worcester, Mass.

Rogers' Wire, Modern Variation 151

Single-strand high tensile strength wire with four-point wire barb. Strand is flattened slightly between barbs. Variation of patent 376418.

Four-point Wire Barbs: *Wrap*

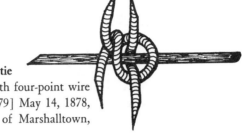

152 Reynolds' Necktie
Single-strand wire with four-point wire
barb. Patented [203779] May 14, 1878,
by Hiram Reynolds of Marshalltown,
Iowa.

**153 Shinn's Barb,
Single-strand Variation**
Single-strand wire with four-point wire
barb. Variation of patent 238447.

**154 Shinn's Barb,
Oval-strand Variation**
Twist-oval wire strand with four-point
wire barb. Variation of patent 238447.

Shinn's Barb, Long-point Variation   155

Single-strand wire with four-point wire barb. Points extend beyond the usual length found in stock fencing. Variation of patent 238447.

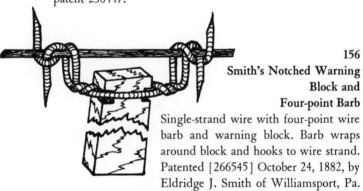

156
Smith's Notched Warning Block and Four-point Barb

Single-strand wire with four-point wire barb and warning block. Barb wraps around block and hooks to wire strand. Patented [266545] October 24, 1882, by Eldridge J. Smith of Williamsport, Pa.

Four-point Wire Barbs: *Twist*

Waco Twist   157

Single-strand wire with four-point wire barb. Strand and barb points are gripped at center and twisted in mounting the barb. Inventor of barb is unknown.

158 Spanner Barb
Single-strand wire with four-point wire barb. Barb parts span the kink and wrap around the strand. Inventor of barb is unknown.

159 Colwell's Saddle Barb
Single-strand kinked wire with four-point wire barb. Twisted two-piece barb straddles the kinked strand. Patented [175667] April 4, 1876, by Myron W. Colwell of Dunlap, Iowa.

160
Allen's Twist
Single-strand wire with four-point wire barb. Wire sections on each side of strand are twisted together to form the barb. Patented [180185] July 25, 1876, by George W. Allen of Creston, Ill.

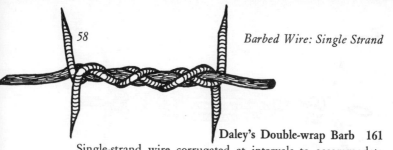

Daley's Double-wrap Barb 161

Single-strand wire corrugated at intervals to accommodate four-point braided wire barbs. Patented [209467] October 29, 1878, by Michael Daley of Waterman, Ill.

Four-point Wire Barbs: *Kink Locked*

Abbott's Australian Kink 162

Single-strand wire with four-point wire barb. Barb is held in position by interlocking loops and kink in the strand. Patented [2308905] January 19, 1943, by Harold Athelstance Abbott of Bendigo, Victoria, Aus.

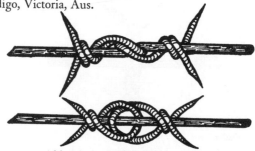

Abbott's Australian Kink, Short Variation 163

Single-strand wire with four-point wire barb. Barb is held in position by interlocking loops and kink in the strand. Variation of patent 2308905.

164 Waco Coils
Single-strand wire with four-point wire barb. Kink in strand
holds barb in position. Inventor of barb is unknown.

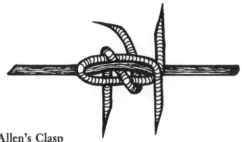

165 Allen's Clasp
Single-strand wire with four-point wire barb. Barb is inter-
locked with kink in wire strand to prevent slippage. Patented
[178581] June 13, 1876, by William G. Allen of Nevada, Iowa.

166 Gunderson's Open-spanner Barb
Single-strand wire with four-point wire barb. Patented
[249173] November 8, 1881, by Albert Gunderson of Shabbona, Ill.

Gunderson's Closed-spanner Barb   167

Single-strand wire with four-point wire barb. Patented
[249173] November 8, 1881, by Albert Gunderson of Shabbona, Ill.

Osterman's Bend   168

Single-strand wire with four-point wire barb. Barb interlocks
with double bend in strand. Patented [268721] December 5,
1882, by John P. Osterman of Joliet, Ill.

Osterman's Simple Bend   169

Single-strand wire with four-point wire barb. Barb interlocks
with double bend in strand. Patented [268721] December 5,
1882, by John P. Osterman of Joliet, Ill.

Four-point Wire Barbs: *Loop Locked*

170 Wilson's Lock
Single-strand wire, four-point barb, and ring. Wire is looped around the two-piece barb parts. Barb is locked in place with a ring. Patented [158451] January 5, 1875, by Francis T. Wilson of Ames, Iowa.

171 Munson's Double "Z"
Single-strand wire with four-point wire barb. Points of barb extend in opposite directions after passing through reverse loops in strand. Patented [214417] April 15, 1879, by Andrew M. Munson of Lee, Ill.

172
Duncan's Triple Tie,
One Strand
Single-strand wire with loop and interlocking four-point wire barb. Patented [218506] August 12, 1879, by John A. Duncan of Kansas City, Mo.

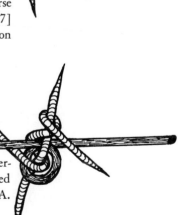

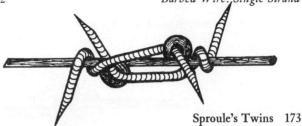

Sproule's Twins   173

Single-strand wire with four-point wire barb. Barb parts pass through loops and wrap around the strand. Patented [275536] April 10, 1883, by Adam W. Sproule of Joliet, Ill.

Four-point Wire Barbs: *Staple*

174
Jayne–Hill's Barb

Single-strand wire with four-point wire barb. Patented [176120] April 11, 1876, by William H. Jayne and James H. Hill of Boone, Iowa.

175
St. John's Locked Staples

Single-strand wire with four-point wire barb. Patented [199330] January 15, 1878, by Spencer H. St. John of Cedar Rapids, Iowa.

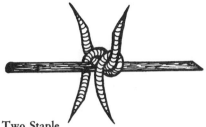

176 Wing's Two Staple
Single-strand wire with four-point wire barb. Patented [200783] February 26, 1878, by Lewis T. Larson Wing of Cambridge, Iowa.

177 Orwig's Crimped Fence Wire
Single-strand fence wire with twin crimps at intervals to hold applicable barbs in position. Patented [201890] April 2, 1878, by Thomas G. Orwig of Des Moines, Iowa.

178 Wilkes' Two Staple
Single-strand wire with four-point wire barb. Patented [216637] June 17, 1879, by Edward V. Wilkes of Kansas City, Mo.

Four-point Wire Barbs: *Block and Nail*

Smith's Spool and Spurs 179

Single-strand wire with wood or cast spools. Nail or wire
spurs are inserted in each spool. Patented [66182] June 25,
1867, by Lucian B. Smith of Kent, Ohio.

Four-point Wire Barbs: *Welded*

Dobbs–Booth's Horn Barb 180

Single-strand wire with four-point wire barb. Horns are
soldered to staple to form the barb. Patented [171104] December 14, 1875, by John Dobbs and Benjamin F. Booth of
Victor, Iowa.

Dobbs–Booth's Curved Horn Barb 181

Single-strand wire with four-point wire barb. Horns are
soldered to staple to form the barb. Patented [171104] December 14, 1875, by John Dobbs and Benjamin F. Booth of
Victor, Iowa.

Four-point Barbs: *Wire and Barbed Washer*

182
Brunner–Reynolds' Four Point
Single-strand wire with staple and two-point, die-cut washer. Patented [200125] February 12, 1878, by Charles Brunner of Peru, and Hiram Reynolds of La Salle, Ill.

Multi-point Barbs: *Coil*

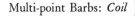

183 Merrill's Six-point Coil
Single-strand wire with six-point wire barb. Pattern of barb changes as the wire is turned. Patented [185688] December 26, 1876, by John C. Merrill of Turkey River Station, Iowa.

184 Merrill's Eight-point Coil
Single-strand wire with eight-point wire barb. Pattern of barb changes as wire is turned. Patented [185688] December 26, 1876, by John C. Merrill of Turkey River Station, Iowa.

Multi-point Barbs: *Spiral Fin*

185

Collins' Single-row Spiraling Barbs

Single-strand wire with spiraling barbs. Barbs are cut and shaped from spiraling rib along the surface of the strand. Patented [173271] February 8, 1876, by William G. Collins of Niles, Ohio.

Collins' Double-row Spiraling Barbs   186

Single-strand wire with spiraling barbs. Barbs are cut and shaped from two rows of spiraling ribs along the surface of the strand. Patented [173271] February 8, 1876, by William G. Collins of Niles, Ohio.

Multi-point Barbs: *Chipped Wire*

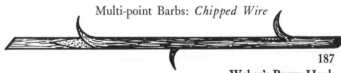

187

Weber's Peavy Hook

Single-strand wire with barbs cut from the same stock. Barbs are channeled out in staggered pattern down the strand. Patented [182976] October 3, 1876, by Theodore A. Weber of New York, N.Y.

Weber's Flat Hook   188

Single-strand wire with barbs cut from the same stock. Barbs are channeled out of flattened areas in a staggered pattern around the strand. Patented [182976] October 3, 1876, by Theodore A. Weber of New York, N.Y.

189 Bagger's Hook
Single-strand wire with barbs cut from the same stock. Barbs
are channeled out of flattened areas in a staggered pattern
around the strand. Patented [183883] October 31, 1876, by
Louis Bagger of Washington, D.C.

Multi-point Barbs: *Sprig*

190 Upham's Grooved Rail and Wire Inserts
Grooved iron rod with one-point wire barb inserts. Patented
[239891] April 5, 1881, by Andrew J. Upham of Sterling, Ill.

Multi-point Barbs: *Welded*

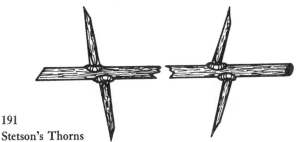

**191
Stetson's Thorns**
Single-strand wire with tack barbs. Paired tacks are soldered
to strand at right angles to adjacent pair. Patented [192468]
June 26, 1877, by Thomas D. Stetson of New York, N.Y.

One-point Sheet Metal Barbs: *Leaf*

Delffs' Tattered Leaf   192
Single-strand wire with irregular-cut, leaf-shaped sheet metal barb. Barbs make fencing visible. Patented [490187] January 17, 1893, by Arnold Delffs of Bedford, Tenn.

Two-point Sheet Metal Barbs: *Coil*

Decker's Ribbed Fence Wire with Sheet Metal Barbs   193
Single-strand ribbed wire showing non-slip advantage of sheet metal barbs pressed into the rib. Patented [178605] June 13, 1876, by Alexander C. Decker of Bushnell, Ill.

Deines' Fence Rod   194
Flat single-strand wire with two-point flat wire barb. Cross-ribs on one side of strand prevent barb slippage. Patented [466775] January 12, 1892, by George Deines of Friend, Nebr.

Two-point Sheet Metal Barbs: *Wrap*

195   Shuman's Blunt Two Point
Single-strand wire with square-cut,
two-point sheet metal barb. Patented
[215404] May 13, 1879, by Thomas
Shuman of Corning, Iowa.

196
Brink's Notched Plate, One Strand
Single-strand wire with two-point sheet metal barb. Patented
[258014] May 16, 1882, by Jacob and Warren M. Brinkerhoff
of Auburn, N.Y.

197
Brink's Butt Plate, One Strand
Single-strand wire with two-point sheet metal barb. Patented
[258014] May 16, 1882, by Jacob and Warren H. Brinkerhoff
of Auburn, N.Y.

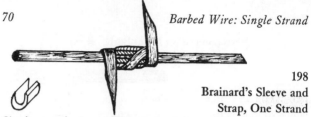

198
Brainard's Sleeve and
Strap, One Strand

Single-strand wire with sheet metal sleeve and two-point barb.
Sleeve is crimped to strand to hold barb in place. Patented
[298440] May 13, 1884, by Curtis B. Brainard of Joliet, Ill.

Two-point Sheet Metal Barbs: *Clip*

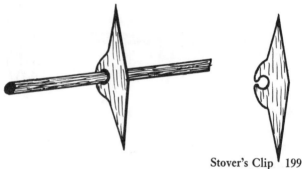

Stover's Clip **199**

Single-strand wire with two-point sheet metal barb. Barb is
mounted by hand. Patented [164947] June 29, 1875, by
Daniel C. Stover of Freeport, Ill.

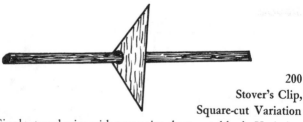

200
Stover's Clip,
Square-cut Variation

Single-strand wire with two-point sheet metal barb. Variation
of patent 164947.

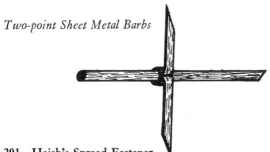

201 Haish's Spread Fastener
Single-strand wire with two-point sheet metal barb. Barb is crimped around the strand. Patented [164552] June 15, 1875, by Jacob Haish of De Kalb, Ill.

202 Haish's Half-spread Fastener
Single-strand wire with two-point sheet metal barb. Patented [164552] June 15, 1875, by Jacob Haish of De Kalb, Ill.

203 Duffy–Schroeder's Grooved Diamond
Single-strand wire with two-point, grooved sheet metal barb. Barb is crimped around strand. Patented [165220] July 6, 1875, by James F. Duffy and Nicholas Schroeder of Chicago, Ill.

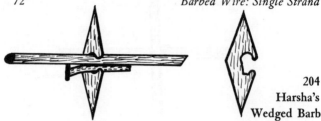

**204
Harsha's
Wedged Barb**

Single-strand wire with two-point sheet metal barb. Barb is keyed to the strand with a metal peg or square nail. Patented [182819] October 3, 1876, by Mortimer S. Harsha of Chicago, Ill.

Two-point Sheet Metal Barbs: *Perforated*

**205
Kelly's
Thorny Fence,
One Strand**

Single-strand wire with curved two-point, diamond-shaped sheet metal barb. Swaged wire prevents barb slippage. Patented [74379] February 11, 1868, by Michael Kelly of New York, N.Y.

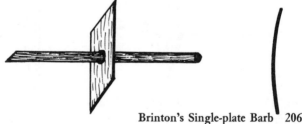

Brinton's Single-plate Barb 206

Single-strand wire with two-point sheet metal barb. Bent plate is straightened to lock in position on strand. Patented [241841] May 24, 1881, by Caleb Brinton of Chicago, Ill.

207
Smallwood's Kink and Shield
Single-strand wire with perforated, two-point sheet metal barb. Strand is kinked to hold barb in place. Patented [254888] March 14, 1882, by Scott Smallwood of Chicago, Ill.

208
Kelly's Swinging Plate
Single-strand wire with two-point sheet metal barb. Barb hangs from an eye twisted in the strand. Patented [322108] July 14, 1885, by Michael Kelly of New York, N.Y.

209 Rogers' Wire with Spindle Barb
Single-strand wire with two-point iron barb. Wire strand is flattened and twisted between the barbs. Patented [376418] January 10, 1888, by Charles D. Rogers of Providence, R.I.

210 Walton's Pivot Barb
Single-strand wire with two-point sheet metal barb alternately staggered at right angles. Assembly consists of slotted wire, barb pin, spring, and block. Spring is fitted in cut block and

both are wedged in the slot. Barb is positioned and locked with pin. Patented [437805] October 7, 1890, by William T. Walton of Mayville, Oreg.

Three-point Sheet Metal Barbs: Wrap

**211
Kennedy's Barb,
Three-point Variation**

Single-strand wire with three-point sheet metal barb. Barb is hand mounted. Variation of patent 153965.

Armstrong's Arrow Point, One Strand   212
Single-strand wire with three-point sheet metal barb. Barb is held in place by lugs and the two points. Patented [182626] September 26, 1876, by Frank Armstrong of Bridgeport, Conn.

Knickerbocker's Barb   213
Single-strand wire with three-point sheet metal barb. Patented

[185333] December 12, 1876, by Millis Knickerbocker of New Lenox, Ill.

214 Brink's Three-point Short Plate
Single-strand wire with three-point sheet metal barb. Long point wraps around strand to hold barb in place. Patented [258706] May 30, 1882, by Jacob and Warren M. Brinkerhoff of Auburn, N.Y.

Three-point Sheet Metal Barbs: *Rider*

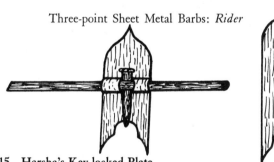

215 Harsha's Key-locked Plate
Single-strand wire with three-point sheet metal barb. Barb is locked on the strand with a pin. Patented [179555] July 4, 1876, by Mortimer S. Harsha of Chicago, Ill.

216 Pooler–Jones' Barb
Single-strand wire with three-point sheet metal barb. Patented [181537] August 27, 1876, by Rheuben H. Pooler and William T. Jones of Serena, Ill.

Barbed Wire: Single Strand

Thompson's Rider Barb   217
Single-strand wire with three-point
sheet metal barb. Barb is held in place
by nicks in strand. Greater weight at
one end keeps barb pointing up.
Patented [233713] October 26, 1880, by
Salmon Thompson of Masonville, Iowa.

Four-point Sheet Metal Barbs: *Wrap*

Kennedy's Barb Plate   218
Single-strand wire with four-point sheet
metal barb. Barb is hand mounted.
Patented [153965] August 11, 1874, by
Charles Kennedy of Hinckley, Ill.

Scutt's Double Clip, One Strand   219
Single-strand wire with four-point sheet metal barb. Offset
cuts in metal plate allow barb points to project at right angles
to each other. Patented [193557] July 24, 1877, by Hiram B.
Scutt of Joliet, Ill.

Four-point Sheet Metal Barbs: *Kink Locked*

220
Dodge's Sheet Metal Barb
Single-strand wire with two-piece, four-point sheet metal
barb. Patented [201507] March 19, 1878, by Thomas H.
Dodge of Worcester, Mass.

221
Dodge's Barbed Ring and Locking Strip
Single-strand wire with four-point sheet metal barb. Kink in
strand holds barbed ring and locking strip in place. Patented
[250899] December 13, 1881, by Thomas H. Dodge of Worcester, Mass.

222
Smallwood's Kink and Star
Single-strand wire with perforated, four-point sheet metal
barb. Strand is kinked to hold barb in place. Patented
[254888] March 14, 1882, by Scott Smallwood of Chicago, Ill.

223

Morgan's Perforated Star

Single-strand kinked wire with four-point, perforated sheet metal barb. Barb is mounted in expansion loop and held in place with wire clip. Patented [302275] July 22, 1884, by Thomas H. Morgan of Pittsburgh, Pa.

Four-point Sheet Metal Barbs: *Joint Locked*

224
Scarlett's
Lug-locked
Barb

Single-strand wire with two-piece, four-point sheet metal barb. The barb parts are bent and friction locked to the strand. Patented [190081] April 24, 1877, by Charles W. and William W. Scarlett, of Aurora, Ill.

225
Scarlett's
Joint-locked
Barb

Single-strand wire with two-piece sheet metal barb. The barb parts are bent and friction locked to the strand. Patented [190081] April 24, 1877, by Charles W. and William W. Scarlett of Aurora, Ill.

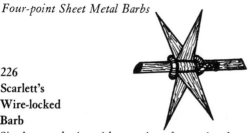

**226
Scarlett's
Wire-locked
Barb**

Single-strand wire with two-piece, four-point sheet metal barb.
The barb parts are bent and wire locked to the strand. Patented
[190081] April 24, 1877, by Charles W. and William W.
Scarlett of Aurora, Ill.

Four-point Sheet Metal Barbs: *Rider*

227   McNeill's Rider

Single-strand wire with four-point sheet metal barb. Barb is
crimped to strand. Patented [199162] January 15, 1878, by
John McNeill of Chicago, Ill.

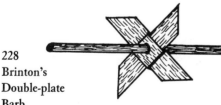

**228
Brinton's
Double-plate
Barb**

Single-strand wire with four-point sheet metal barb. Bent
plates are straightened to lock in position on strand. Patented
[241841] May 24, 1881, by Caleb Brinton of Chicago, Ill.

Four-point Sheet Metal Barbs: *Star*

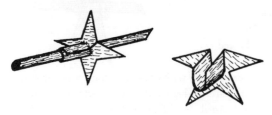

Kennedy's Socket Barb   229

Single-strand wire with pre-formed, four-point sheet metal
barb. Barb is hand mounted. Patented [153965] August 11,
1874, by Charles Kennedy of Hinckley, Ill.

Ellwood's Star   230

Single-strand wire and four-point star barb. Barb and wire
are formed from the same material. Patented [163169] May
11, 1875, by Reuben Ellwood of Sycamore, Ill.

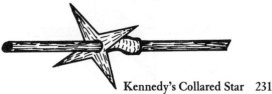

Kennedy's Collared Star   231

Single-strand wire with four-point sheet metal barb. Barb is
held in place by crimp in wire strand and barb collar. Patented
[164181] June 8, 1875, by Charles Kennedy of Hinckley, Ill.

Four-point Sheet Metal Barbs: *Spinner*

232 Lord's Spinner, One Strand
Single-strand wire with four-point sheet metal barb. Diamond-shaped barb plates are joined by a shaft through the looped strand and rotate under load. Patented [218290] August 5, 1879, by Tylor C. Lord of Joliet, Ill.

Multi-point Sheet Metal Barbs: *Star*

233 Kennedy's Five-point Star
Single-strand wire with five-point sheet metal barb. Barb is hand mounted. Patented [153965] August 11, 1874, by Charles Kennedy of Hinckley, Ill.

234 Kennedy's Six-point Star
Single-strand wire with six-point sheet metal barb. Barb is hand mounted. Patented [153965] August 11, 1874, by Charles Kennedy of Hinckley, Ill.

Dodge's Spur Wheel   235

Single-strand wire with six-point sheet metal barb. Barb rotates between splined areas in strand. Patented [250219] November 29, 1881, by Thomas H. Dodge of Worcester, Mass.

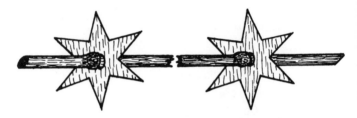

Olsen's Swaged-spur Wheel   236

Single-strand wire with six-point sheet metal barb. Barb is held in position by swaged areas in strand. Patented [251276] December 20, 1881, by Olaf R. Olsen of Indianapolis, Ind.

Sjöström's Joined-saucer Barb   237

Single-strand wire with six-point sheet metal barb. Joined halves are folded together and strung side by side on wire strand. Patented [387116] July 31, 1888, by Johannes Sjöström of Gefle, Swed.

238 Sjöström's Saucer Barb

Single-strand wire with twelve-point sheet metal barb. Separate halves of barb are clustered face to face on wire strand. Patented [387116] July 31, 1888, by Johannes Sjöström of Gefle, Swed.

Multi-point Sheet Metal Barbs: *Wheel*

239 Hunt's Spur Wheel

Single-strand wire with fourteen-point sheet metal spur wheel. Wheel is held in place with sheet metal tabs. Patented [67117] July 23, 1867, by William D. Hunt of Scott, N.Y.

240 Barker's Spur Wheel, One Strand

Single-strand wire with twelve-point sheet metal barb. Barb rotates on wire shaft fastened to wire strands. Patented [251505] December 27, 1881, by George E. Barker of Waverly, N.Y.

Multi-point Sheet Metal Barbs: *Sprig*

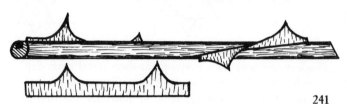

241

Upham's Grooved Rail and Double-point Inserts

Grooved iron rod with two-point sheet metal barb inserts. Patented [239891] April 5, 1881, by Andrew J. Upham of Sterling, Ill.

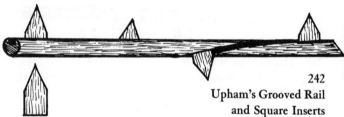

242

Upham's Grooved Rail and Square Inserts

Grooved iron rod with pointed square sheet metal barb inserts. Patented [239891] April 5, 1881, by Andrew J. Upham of Sterling, Ill.

243·

Upham's Grooved Rail and Triangle Inserts

Grooved iron rod with triangle sheet metal barb inserts. Patented [239891] April 5, 1881, by Andrew J. Upham of Sterling, Ill.

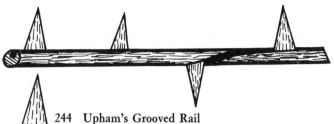

**244   Upham's Grooved Rail
and Long Triangle Inserts**

Grooved iron rod with triangle sheet metal barb inserts.
Patented [239891] April 5, 1881, by Andrew J. Upham of
Sterling, Ill.

Multi-point Sheet Metal Barbs: *Strand-mounted Barb Strips*

245   Hallner's Wrap, Single Cut
Single-strand wire with wrap-around sheet metal strip. Cuts
along one edge of strip form the barbs. Patented [199538]
January 22, 1878, by John Hallner of Ithaca, Nebr.

246   Hallner's Wrap, Double Cut
Single-strand wire with wrap-around sheet metal strip. Cuts
along edges of strip form the barbs. Patented [199538] January 22, 1878, by John Hallner of Ithaca, Nebr.

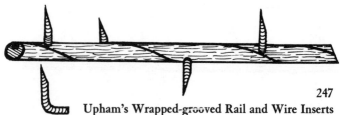

247

Upham's Wrapped-grooved Rail and Wire Inserts
Grooved iron rod with wire barb inserts. Barbs are wedged in groove and the rod wrapped with a spiraling metallic strip. Patented [239892] April 5, 1881, by Andrew J. Upham of Sterling, Ill.

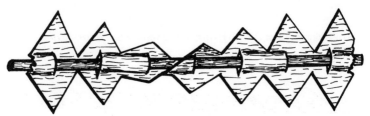

Brock's Diamond Chain   248
Single-strand wire with a strip of diamond-shaped sheet metal barbs. Wire runs through openings formed by alternate depressions in sheet metal strip. Patented [255763] April 4, 1882, by William E. Brock of New York, N.Y.

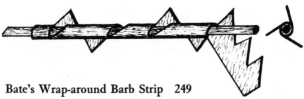

Bate's Wrap-around Barb Strip   249
Single-strand wire wrapped with spiraling serrated strip. Patented [273245] March 6, 1883, by William S. Bate of Boston, Mass.

250 Blackmer's Strip and Tack

Single-strand wire wrapped with tack-studded sheet metal strip. Patented [305276] September 16, 1884, by Francis A. Blackmer of Springfield, Mass.

251 Upham's Barb and Lap

Single-wire strand and sheet metal strip with projecting points. Alternate points are crimped around the wire. Patented [305355] September 16, 1884, by Andrew J. Upham of Sterling, Ill.

Multi-point Sheet Metal Barbs: *Disc*

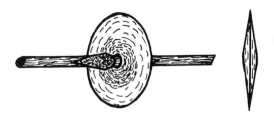

252 Neely–Marland's Disc

Single-strand wire with knife-edge, circular sheet metal barb. Patented [251273] December 20, 1881, by Thomas Neely and Alfred Marland of Pittsburgh, Pa.

BARBED WIRE: Two Strand

One-point Wire Barbs: *Wrap*

Huffman's Visible Round-wire Fencing 253

Two single-wire strands with one-point wire barbs. Wire is stapled to wooden stays between posts to keep barbs pointing down. Patented [380573] April 3, 1888, by Orlando Huffman of Friend, Nebr.

254
Huffman's Visible Flat-wire Fencing

Two flattened wire strands with one-point, round-wire barbs. Wire is stapled to wooden stays between posts to keep barbs pointing down. Patented [418617] December 31, 1889, by Orlando Huffman of Friend, Nebr.

Huffman's Barb, Small Parallel Variation 255

Two flattened parallel strands with one-point, round-wire barb. Variation of patent 418617.

One-point Wire Barbs: *Block and Nail*

256 Hulbert's Block and Spike, Nail Variation
Two-strand wire with block and one-point nail barb. Variation of patent 296835.

Two-point Wire Barbs: *Single Turn*

257 Blount Two Point
Two-strand wire with two-point wire barb. Inventor of barb is unknown.

258 La Crosse Barb
Two-strand wire with two-point wire barbs. Barbs are alternately mounted on the strands. Inventor of barb is unknown.

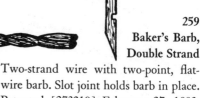

259
Baker's Barb,
Double Strand
Two-strand wire with two-point, flat-wire barb. Slot joint holds barb in place. Patented [273219] February 27, 1883, by George C. Baker of Des Moines, Iowa.

260
Baker's Barb, Perfect Variation
Two-strand wire with two-point, flat-wire barb. Variation of patent 273219.

261
Baker's Barb,
Needle-point Variation
Two-strand wire with two-point, flat-wire barb. Variation of patent 273219.

262
Baker's Barb,
Blunt Variation
Two-strand wire with two-point, flat-wire barb. Barb has one split and one rounded point. Variation of patent 273219.

263
Baker's Barb, Large–Small-strand Variation
Two-strand wire with two-point, flat-wire barb. Barb is
mounted on the smaller strand. Variation of patent 273219.

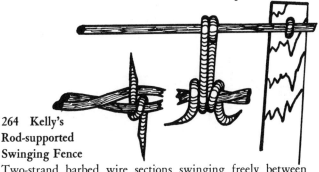

**264 Kelly's
Rod-supported
Swinging Fence**
Two-strand barbed wire sections swinging freely between
posts on barbed linkage. Links hang from rods stapled to
posts. Patented [283614] August 21, 1883, by Michael Kelly of
New York, N.Y.

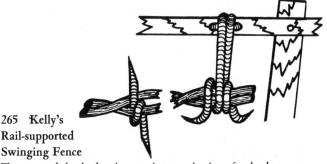

**265 Kelly's
Rail-supported
Swinging Fence**
Two-strand barbed wire sections swinging freely between
posts on barbed linkage. Links hang from staples in wooden
rail nailed to posts. Patented [283614] August 21, 1883, by
Michael Kelly of New York, N.Y.

266
Edenborn's Wrap Barb
Twisted web wire with two-point wire
barb. Barb wraps around the webbed
strand. Patented [313929] March 17,
1885, by William Edenborn of St. Louis,
Mo.

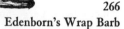

267
Edenborn's Outside Barb
Twisted web wire with two-point wire
barb. Barb passes through the thin web.
Patented [313929] March 17, 1885, by
William Edenborn of St. Louis, Mo.

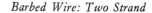

268
Edenborn's Wrap Barb,
Modern Variation
Two-strand high tensile strength wire
with two-point wire barb. Variation of
patent 313929.

269
Edenborn's Wrap Barb,
Double-strand Variation
Two-strand wire with two-point wire
barb. Barb wraps around both strands.
Variation of patent 313929.

270 Haish's Single-wrap Ribbed Barb
Two-strand wire with two-point, half-round wire barb. Barb
is wrapped around one strand and is held in position by teeth
in flat surface. Patented [356762] February 1, 1887, by Jacob
Haish of De Kalb, Ill.

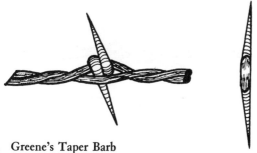

271 Greene's Taper Barb
Two-strand wire with two-point, tapered-wire barb. Barb is
held in place by flat central surface. Patented [380884] April
10, 1888, by Merritt Greene of Marshalltown, Iowa.

272 Haish's Spear Point
Two-strand wire with shaped two-point barb. Flattened body
of barb prevents rotation. Patented [463742] November 24,
1891, by Jacob Haish of De Kalb, Ill.

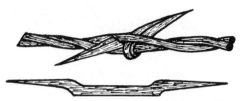

Haish's Cleat   273

Two-strand wire with shaped, two-point wire barb. Body of
barb is flattened to prevent rotation. Patented [463742] November 24, 1891, by Jacob Haish of De Kalb, Ill.

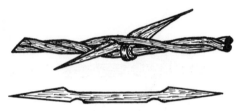

Haish's Notched Spear Point   274

Two-strand wire with shaped, two-point wire barb. Body of
barb is flattened and notched to prevent rotation. Patented
[463742] November 24, 1891, by Jacob Haish of De Kalb, Ill.

Curtis' Quarter Twist   275

Two-strand wire with two-point, half-round barb. A quarter
turn is made in each barb point. Patented [470746] March 15,
1892, by John D. Curtis of Worcester, Mass.

276 Curtis' Barb, Flat-strand Variation
Two-strand flattened wire with two-point, half-round wire barb. Variation of patent 470746.

277 Haish's Single Wrap, Modern Waukegan Variation
Two-strand wire with two-point, half-round barb. Variation of patent 470746.

278 Curtis' Half Twist
Two-strand wire with two-point, half-round barb. A half turn is made in each barb point. Patented [470747] March 15, 1892, by John D. Curtis of Worcester, Mass.

Riter's Visible Wire with Barbs   279

Two-strand fence wire with two-point wire barbs. Fencing
consists of alternating sections of loose and tight twists.
Patented [506256] October 10, 1893, by John L. Riter of
Brownsville, Ind.

Smith's Beads and Barbs   280

Two-strand visible wire with two-point wire barbs. The two
barbs alternate with bead-shaped open spreads. Patented
[578032] March 2, 1897, by Datus C. Smith of Yonkers, N.Y.

Perry's Welded Barb, Double Strand   281

Two-strand wire with two-point wire barbs. Barbs are electrically welded to one strand. Patented [588774] August 24,
1897, by John C. Perry of Joliet, Ill.

282 Perry's Welded Barb, Double-strand Wrap-around
Two-strand wire with two-point wire barbs. Barbs are electrically welded in position. Patented [588774] August 24, 1897, by John C. Perry of Joliet, Ill.

Two-point Wire Barbs: *Coil*

283 Vertical Spiral Barb
Two-strand wire with two-point wire barb. Body of barb overlaps and coils outward from the strand. Inventor of barb is unknown.

284 Modern Spring Coil
Two-strand wire with two-point flat steel barb. Barb coils outward from strand. Inventor of barb is unknown.

Glidden's Coil, Double Strand   285

Two-strand wire with two-point wire barb. Barb coil consists
of three or more turns. Patent reissue [6913] February 8, 1876,
by Joseph F. Glidden of De Kalb, Ill.

Glidden's Coil, Spread Strand   286

Two crossing single-wire strands with two-point wire barb.
Barb coil consists of three or more turns. Patent reissue [6913]
February 8, 1876, by Joseph F. Glidden of De Kalb, Ill.

Glidden's Coil, Hanging-barb Variation   287

Two-strand wire with two-point wire barbs. Points on each
barb extend in the same direction. Variation of reissue patent
6913.

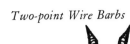

288 Glidden's Coil, Military-wire Variation

Two-strand military entanglement wire with two-point wire barbs. Barb points are staggered around the wire strands. Variation of reissue patent 6913.

289 Glidden's Barb, Modern Reversing-twist Variation

Two-strand high tensile strength wire with two-point, flat-wire barb. Strands twist in opposite directions away from barb. Variation of reissue patent 6913.

290 Glidden's Winner

Two-strand wire with two-point wire barb. Barb makes double turn around one strand. Patented [157124] November 24, 1874, by Joseph F. Glidden of De Kalb, Ill.

291 Glidden's Barb, Common Variation

Two-strand wire with two-point wire barb. Variation of patent 157124.

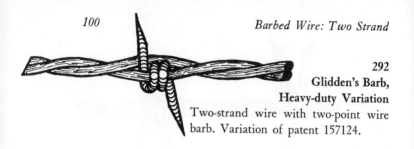

292
Glidden's Barb,
Heavy-duty Variation
Two-strand wire with two-point wire
barb. Variation of patent 157124.

293
Glidden's Barb,
Large–Small-strand Variation
Two-strand wire with two-point wire
barb. Barb is mounted on the larger
strand. Variation of patent 157124.

294
Glidden's Barb,
Flat-strand Variation
Two-strand wire with two-point wire
barb. Wire strands are of different
gauge. Smaller strand is half-flattened.
Variation of patent 157124.

295
Glidden's Barb,
Small Double-strand,
Square-wire Variation
Two-strand spiraling square wire with
two-point wire barb. Variation of patent
157124.

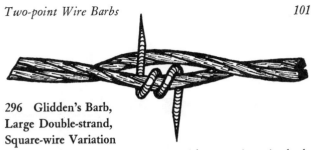

**296 Glidden's Barb,
Large Double-strand,
Square-wire Variation**
Two-strand spiraling square wire with two-point wire barb.
Variation of patent 157124.

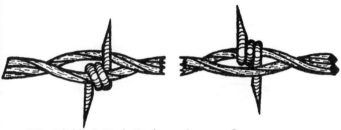

**297 Glidden's Barb, Barbs on Separate Square
Strands Variation**
Two-strand spiraling square wire with two-point wire barb
on each strand. Variation of patent 157124.

298 Glidden's Barb, Round–Square-wire Variation
Two-strand wire with two-point wire barb. Wire strands con-
sist of one round and one spiraling square wire. Variation of
patent 157124.

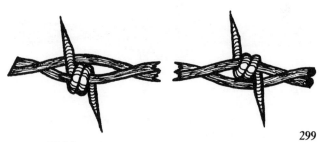

299

Glidden's Barb, Barbs on Alternate Strands Variation
Two-strand wire with two-point wire barbs. Barbs appear on
alternate strands. Variation of patent 157124.

300

Glidden's Barb, Four-strand Cable Variation
Cable and single-strand wire with two-point wire barb. Barb
is mounted on the wire strand. Variation of patent 157124.

301

Glidden's Barb, Five-strand Cable Variation
Cable and single-strand wire with two-point wire barb. Barb
is mounted on the wire strand. Variation of patent 157124.

302
Glidden's Barb, Barbed Five-strand Cable Variation
Cable and single-strand wire with two-point wire barb. Barb
is mounted on the cable. Variation of patent 157124.

303
Glidden's Barb, Six-strand Cable Variation
Cable and single-strand wire with two-point wire barb. Barb
is mounted on the cable. Variation of patent 157124.

304
Glidden's Barb, Seven-strand Cable Variation
Cable and single-strand wire with two-point wire barb. Barb
is mounted on the cable. Variation of patent 157124.

Glidden's Barb, Visible Wire Variation   305
Separate undulating wire strands with two-point wire barbs.
Barbs wrap around both strands at points of contact. Varia-
tion of patent 157124.

306
Glidden's Barb, Modern
Half-round Barb Variation
Two-strand aluminum alloy wire with
two-point, half-round wire barb. Varia-
tion of patent 157124.

307
Glidden's Barb, Modern
Aluminum Alloy Variation
Two-strand aluminum alloy wire and
two-point barb. Variation of patent
157124.

308
Glidden's Barb,
Triangle–Round-strand
Variation
Two-strand wire with two-point wire
barb. Fencing consists of one triangle
and one round strand. Barb is mounted
on the round strand. Variation of patent
157124.

309
Glidden's Barb,
Square–Oval-strand Variation
Two-strand wire with two-point wire
barb. Fencing consists of one oval and
one square strand. Barb is mounted on
the square strand. Variation of patent
157124.

310
Glidden's Barb,
Flat-barb Variation
Two-strand wire with two-point sheet
metal barb. Variation of patent 157124.

311
Glidden's Barb,
Large–Small-strand Variation
Small and large wire strands with two-
point wire barb. Barb is mounted on the
smaller wire. Variation of patent 157124.

312
Glidden's Barb,
Flat Variation
Two-strand wire with two-point, flat-
wire barb. Variation of patent 157124.

313
Glidden's Barb, Cactus-point Variation

Two-strand wire with two-point wire barb. Variation of patent 157124.

314
Glidden's Barb, Square-barb Variation

Two-strand wire with two-point, square-wire barb. Variation of patent 157124.

315
Upham's Outside Coil

Two-strand wire with two-point wire coil barb. Patented [205702] July 2, 1878, by Andrew J. Upham of Sterling, Ill.

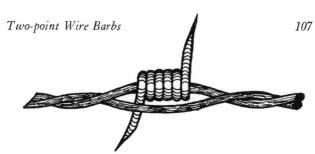

316 Wright's Rotating Coil

Two-strand wire with two-point wire coil barb. Large opening through coil allows barb to turn under load. Patented [249817] November 22, 1881, by Ivy E. Wright of Charlottesville, Ind.

**317 Dodge's Conductor, Copper-steel
Wire and Copper Barb**

Copper and steel wire lightning conductor with two-point copper wire barb. Barb is mounted on the copper wire strand. Patented [282449] July 31, 1883, by Thomas H. Dodge of Worcester, Mass.

**318 Dodge's Conductor, Double Copper
Strand and Steel Barb Variation**

Two-strand copper wire lightning conductor with two-point steel wire barb. Variation of patent 282449.

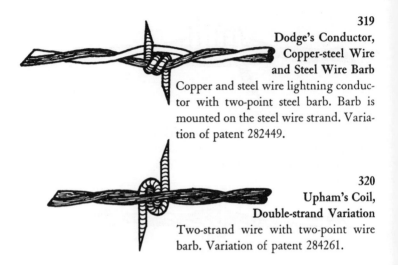

319
Dodge's Conductor,
Copper-steel Wire
and Steel Wire Barb
Copper and steel wire lightning conductor with two-point steel barb. Barb is mounted on the steel wire strand. Variation of patent 282449.

320
Upham's Coil,
Double-strand Variation
Two-strand wire with two-point wire barb. Variation of patent 284261.

321
Edenborn's Single-straddle Barb
Twisted web wire with two-point wire barb. Barb passes through the thin web. Patented [313929] March 17, 1885, by William Edenborn of St. Louis, Mo.

322
Edenborn's Straddle Barb,
Double-strand Variation
Two-strand wire with two-point wire barb. Variation of patent 313929.

Two-point Wire Barbs: *Wrap*

323
Double Turn and Wrap Barb
Two-strand wire with two-point wire barb. Inventor of barb is unknown.

324 Haish's "S"
Two-strand wire with two-point wire barb. Patented [167240] August 31, 1875, by Jacob Haish of De Kalb, Ill.

325 Haish's "S,"
Square Variation
Two-strand wire with two-point wire barb. Variation of patent 167240.

Haish's "S," Wrap Variation   326

Two-strand wire with two-point wire barb. Variation of patent 167240.

Haish's "S," Parallel Variation   327

Two parallel single-wire strands with two-point wire barb. Variation of patent 167240.

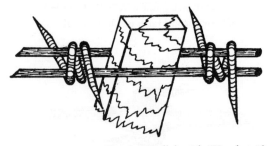

Frye's Parallel with Wooden Slat   328

Parallel single-wire strands with two-point wire barbs. Slats keep barb points in horizontal position. Patented [204312] May 8, 1878, by William H. H. Frye of Marshalltown, Iowa.

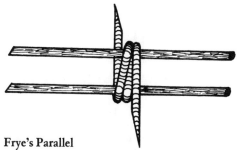

329 Frye's Parallel
Parallel single-wire strands with two-point wire barb. Patented [204312] May 8, 1878, by William H. H. Frye of Marshalltown, Iowa.

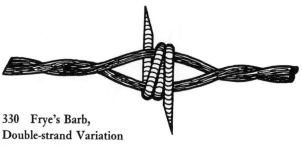

**330 Frye's Barb,
Double-strand Variation**
Two-strand wire with two-point wire barb. Variation of patent 204312.

331 Brotherton's Barb
Two-strand wire with two-point wire barb. Patented [207710] September 3, 1878, by Jacob Brotherton of Ames, Iowa.

Brotherton's Barb, Common Variation   332

Two-strand wire with two-point wire barb. Variation of patent 207710.

Brotherton's Barb, Arched-strand Variation   333

Two-strand wire with two-point wire barb. Barb is locked in place by sharp bend in one strand. Variation of patent 207710.

Brotherton's Barb, Free Wrap Variation   334

Two-strand wire with two-point wire barb. Variation of patent 207710.

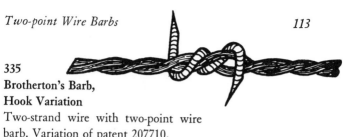

335
Brotherton's Barb,
Hook Variation
Two-strand wire with two-point wire
barb. Variation of patent 207710.

336
Vaughan's Triple Loop
Two-strand wire with two-point wire
barb. Patented [212874] March 4, 1879,
by Henry M. Vaughan of Newton,
Iowa.

337
Edenborn's Flat "S"
Twisted web wire with two-point wire
barb. Barb passes through the thin web.
Patented [313929] March 17, 1885, by
William Edenborn of St. Louis, Mo.

338
Edenborn's Point Lock
Twisted web wire with two-point wire
barb. Barb passes through the thin web.
Patented [313929] March 17, 1885, by
William Edenborn of St. Louis, Mo.

Edenborn's "S"   339

Twisted web wire with two-point wire barb. Barb passes through the thin web. Patented [313929] March 17, 1885, by William Edenborn of St. Louis, Mo.

Edenborn's Vertical Point   340

Twisted web wire with two-point wire barb. Barb passes through the thin web. Patented [313929] March 17, 1885, by William Edenborn of St. Louis, Mo.

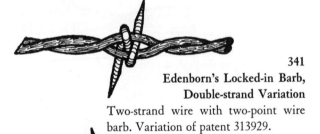

341
Edenborn's Locked-in Barb,
Double-strand Variation

Two-strand wire with two-point wire barb. Variation of patent 313929.

342
Edenborn's Point Lock,
Double-strand Variation

Two-strand wire with two-point wire barb. Variation of patent 313929.

**343   Edenborn's Point Lock,
Parallel-strand Variation**
Two parallel single-wire strands with two-point wire barb.
Variation of patent 313929.

Two-point Wire Barbs: *Kink Locked*

**344   Ford's Kink and Twist,
Double Strand**
Two-strand wire with two-point wire barb. Strands are kinked to receive twisted barb. Patented [311740] February 3, 1884, by Franklin D. Ford of Providence, R.I.

**345   Ford's Kink and Wrap Barb,
Double Strand**
Two-strand wire with two-point wire barb. Strands are bent at intervals to hold barbs in place. Patented [312454] February 17, 1885, by Franklin D. Ford of Providence, R.I.

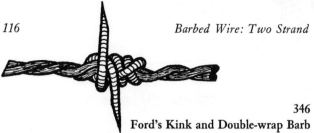

346
Ford's Kink and Double-wrap Barb
Two-strand wire with two-point wire barb. Strands are bent
at intervals to hold barbs in place. Patented [312454] February 17, 1885, by Franklin D. Ford of Providence, R.I.

Two-point Wire Barbs: *Loop Locked*

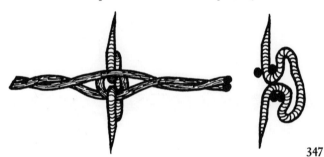

347
Pitney's Loop and Fastener
Barb, Double Strand
Two-strand wire with two-point bent
wire barb. One strand loops around barb
to hold it in place. Patented [208538]
October 1, 1878, by Albert L. Pitney of
Washington, D.C.

Hepp's Loop and Staple   348
Two-strand wire with two-point wire
barb. Loop in one strand holds barb in
place. Patented [249522] November 15,
1881, by David Hepp of Chicago, Ill.

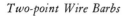

349 Evans' Two-point Tie

Two-strand wire with one strand in sections twisted at ends to form eyes and barbs. Barb points pass through eyes to join wire sections. Patented [255728] March 28, 1882, by Lemuel E. Evans of East Orange, N.J.

350 Weber's Paired Loops

Two-strand wire with two-point wire barb. Interlocking loops are formed in one strand to hold barb. Patented [286512] October 9, 1883, by Theodore A. Weber of New York, N.Y.

351 Kelly's Swinging Barb, Double Strand

Two-strand wire with two-point wire barb. Barb hangs from loop in one strand. Patented [322108] July 14, 1885, by Michael Kelly of New York, N.Y.

352
Potter's Controlled Points

Two-strand wire with two-point wire barb. Barb is formed from one strand and tied with the other. Loops limit the distance that barb points extend. Patented [331908] December 8, 1885, by James Potter of Chicago, Ill.

Potter's Controlled Points, Loop Strand   353

Two-strand wire with two-point wire barb. One strand of wire loops around and holds barb in place. Patented [336664] February 23, 1886, by James Potter of Chicago, Ill.

Two-point Wire Barbs: *Washer Locked*

354
Vosburgh's Washer-locked Barb, Double Strand

Two-strand wire with two-point wire barb. Arched barb is locked in place with a slotted metal plate between the strands. Patented [182778] October 3, 1876, by Cyrus A. Vosburgh of Chicago, Ill.

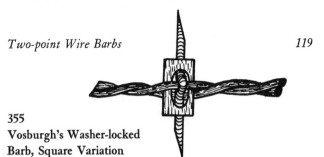

355
Vosburgh's Washer-locked
Barb, Square Variation
Two-strand wire with two-point wire barb. Arched barb is locked in place with a slotted metal plate between the strands. Variation of patent 182778.

356
Whiteman's Washer-locked Barb
Two-strand wire with one strand composed of wire sections joined at ends to form two-point barbs. Barb points are washer locked. Patented [248374] October 18, 1881, by Israel R. Whiteman of Chicago, Ill.

Two-point Wire Barbs: *Clip*

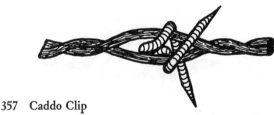

357   Caddo Clip
Two-strand wire with two-point wire barb. Strands grip the barb and are locked in place by the barb points. Strands twist in opposite directions away from the barb. Inventor of barb is unknown.

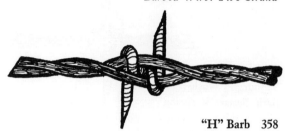

"H" Barb   358

Two-strand wire with two-point wire barb. Loop in barb lies
between the strands. Inventor of barb is unknown.

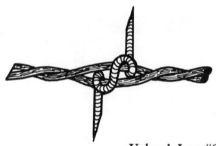

Upham's Lazy "S"   359

Two-strand wire with two-point, clip-on wire barb. Patented
[205702] July 2, 1878, by Andrew J. Upham of Sterling, Ill.

St. John's Fastener   360

Two-strand wire with two-point wire barb. Patented [249418]
November 8, 1881, by Spencer H. St. John of Cedar Rapids,
Iowa.

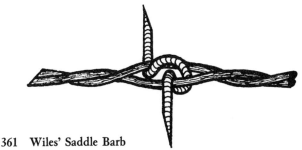

361 Wiles' Saddle Barb
Two-strand wire with bent wire barb. Patented [257196]
May 2, 1882, by Robert H. Wiles of Freeport, Ill.

362 Upham's Saddle Barb
Two-strand wire with two-point coiled wire barb. Patented
[264495] September 19, 1882, by Andrew J. Upham of Sterling, Ill.

363 Evans' Fastener
Two-strand wire with two-point interlocking wire barb.
Patented [267067] November 7, 1882, by Lemuel E. Evans
of East Orange, N.J.

364

**Brainerd's Retainer
Plate and Barb**

Two-strand wire with two-point wire barb. Barb is held in place by retaining plate gripping both strands. Patented [314512] March 24, 1885, by Frank W. Brainerd of Chicago, Ill.

365

Hill's Clip, Double Strand

Two-strand wire with two-point wire barb. Clip-shaped barb is crimped to both strands. Patented [330893] November 24, 1885, by Christian C. Hill of Chicago, Ill.

366

Hill's Clip, Parallel Strand

Two parallel wire strands with two-point wire barb. Clip-shaped barb is crimped to both strands. Patented [330893] November 24, 1885, by Christian C. Hill of Chicago, Ill.

367 Scutt's Crimp
Two-strand wire with two-point wire barb. Bent body holds
barb in place. Patented [332755] December 22, 1885, by
Hiram B. Scutt of Joliet, Ill.

368 Kraft's Crimp, Double Strand
Two-strand wire with two-point wire barb. Barb and one
strand are crimped to hold barb in place. Patented [341921]
May 18, 1886, by Charles J. F. Kraft and Augustus C. H.
Kraft of Joliet, Ill.

Two-point Wire Barbs: *Spreader*

369 Upham's Figure-eight Tie
Two-strand wire with two-point wire barb. Barb points are
perpendicular to spread strands. Strands are twisted so that
each succeeding barb is turned 90 degrees. Patented [181608]
August 29, 1876, by Andrew J. Upham of Sterling, Ill.

370

McNeill's Snake Tongue Parallel
Two parallel single-wire strands with auger-pointed wire barbs. Patented [189122] April 3, 1877, by John McNeill of Chicago, Ill.

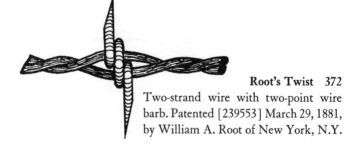

Root's Spread   371
Two-strand wire with two-point wire barb. Patented [239553] March 29, 1881, by William A. Root of New York, N.Y.

Root's Twist   372
Two-strand wire with two-point wire barb. Patented [239553] March 29, 1881, by William A. Root of New York, N.Y.

373
Root's Spread, Reverse Points Variation
Two-strand wire with two-point wire barb. Barb points make one and a half turns around the wire strands. Variation of patent 239553.

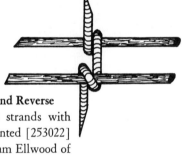

374 Ellwood's Parallel and Reverse
Two parallel single-wire strands with two-point wire barb. Patented [253022] January 31, 1882, by Abram Ellwood of Sycamore, Ill.

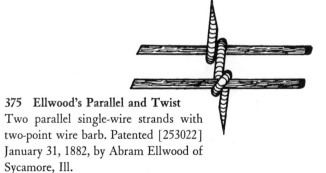

375 Ellwood's Parallel and Twist
Two parallel single-wire strands with two-point wire barb. Patented [253022] January 31, 1882, by Abram Ellwood of Sycamore, Ill.

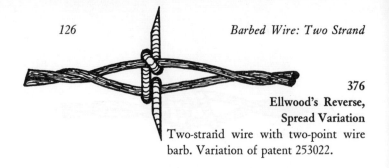

376
Ellwood's Reverse,
Spread Variation
Two-strand wire with two-point wire
barb. Variation of patent 253022.

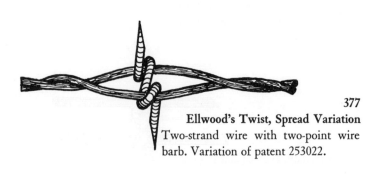

377
Ellwood's Twist, Spread Variation
Two-strand wire with two-point wire
barb. Variation of patent 253022.

Miles' Parallel and Spear Points   378
Two parallel single-wire strands joined
by crossing wire extending in loops at
each joint. Loops are shaped into spear-
point barbs. Patented [277917] May 22,
1883, by Purches Miles of Brooklyn,
N.Y.

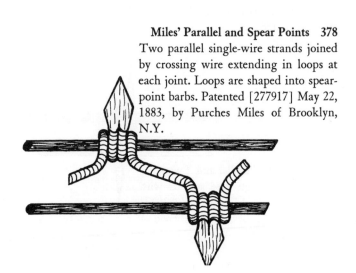

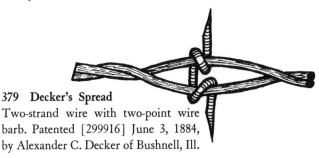

379 Decker's Spread
Two-strand wire with two-point wire
barb. Patented [299916] June 3, 1884,
by Alexander C. Decker of Bushnell, Ill.

**380 Decker's Barb, Narrow
Parallel-strand Variation**
Two parallel single-wire strands with
two-point wire barb. Variation of patent
299916.

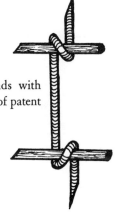

**381 Decker's Barb, Wide
Parallel-strand Variation**
Two parallel single-wire strands with
two-point wire barb. Variation of patent
299916.

382
Nadelhoffer's Round-wire Gull Wing

Two-strand wire with two-point wire barb. Patented [307673] November 4, 1884, by John Nadelhoffer of Joliet, Ill.

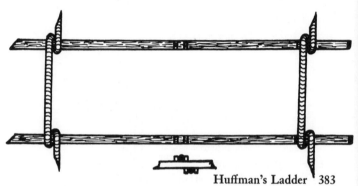

Huffman's Ladder **383**

Two flattened, parallel single-wire strands with two-point wire barbs. Offset lugs extending from flat surfaces hold barb in place. Patented [442525] December 9, 1890, by Orlando Huffman of Friend, Nebr.

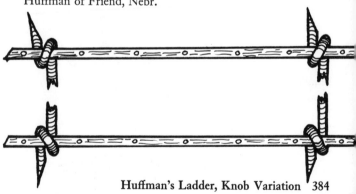

Huffman's Ladder, Knob Variation **384**

Two flattened, parallel single-wire strands with two-point

wire barbs. Knobs projecting from flat surfaces hold barb in place. Variation of patent 442525.

Two-point Wire Barbs: *Horizontal Strand Locking*

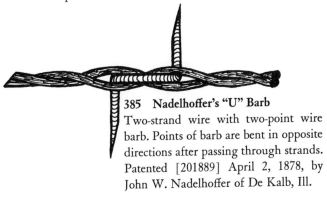

385   Nadelhoffer's "U" Barb
Two-strand wire with two-point wire barb. Points of barb are bent in opposite directions after passing through strands. Patented [201889] April 2, 1878, by John W. Nadelhoffer of De Kalb, Ill.

386
Nadelhoffer's "U" Barb, Spread-point Variation
Two-strand wire with two-point wire barb. Spreading points and tight twist hold barb in place. Variation of patent 201889.

387   Baker and Bestor's Staple Barb
Two-strand wire with two-point bent wire barb. Patented [208140] September 17, 1878, by Charles H. Baker and Francis L. Bestor of Oskaloosa, Iowa.

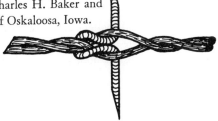

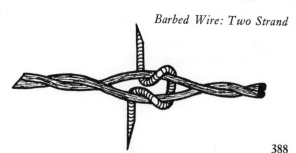

388

Baker and Bestor's Staple Barb, Spread Variation
Two-strand wire with spread, two-point bent wire barb.
Variation of patent 208140.

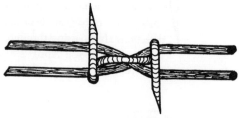

Nadelhoffer's Crossover   389
Two single-wire strands with two-point wire barbs. Strands
are crossed and fastened with barbs at regular intervals.
Patented [270098] January 2, 1883, by John W. Nadelhoffer
of Naperville, Ill.

390

Nadelhoffer's Crossover, Twist-strand Variation
Two-strand wire with two-point wire barbs. Strands cross
under each barb. Variation of patent 270098.

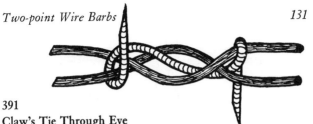

391
Claw's Tie Through Eye
Two single strands of wire with interlocking, two-point wire barb. Patented [285014] September 18, 1883, by William M. Claw of Wheatland, Ill.

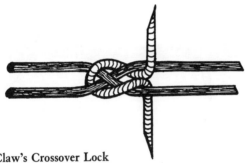

392   Claw's Crossover Lock
Two wire strands crossing at intervals and locked in place with two-point wire barbs. Patented [287803] November 6, 1883, by William M. Claw of Wheatland, Ill.

Two-point Wire Barbs: *Dropped Loop*

393   Brainard's Dropped Loop
Two-strand wire with two-point wire barb. Barb is looped to provide attachment for warning devices. Patented [268453] December 5, 1882, by Curtis B. Brainard of Joliet, Ill.

394
Brainard's Dropped Loop,
Hanging Variation

Two-strand wire with looped two-point wire barb. Variation of patent 268453.

Blake's Body Grip   395

Two-strand wire with two-point wire barb. Flattened surfaces in body of barb are gripped by strands to hold barb in position. Patented [446607] February 17, 1891, by John W. Blake of Marshall, Minn.

Two-point Wire Barbs: *Tie*

Emerson's Loop and Double Wire   396

Two single-wire strands with two-point wire barb. Strands are kinked to hold barb in place. Patented [176523] April 25, 1876, by Richard Emerson of Sycamore, Ill.

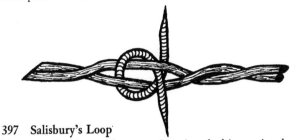

397 Salisbury's Loop

Two-strand wire with two-point, interlocking wire barb. Patented [177752] May 23, 1876, by Charles H. Salisbury of De Kalb, Ill.

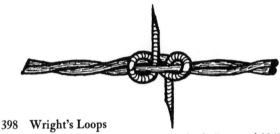

398 Wright's Loops

Two-strand wire with two-point wire barb. Patented [245256] August 2, 1881, by Ivy E. Wright of Charlottesville, Ind.

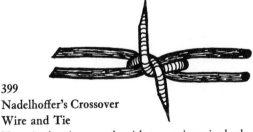

**399
Nadelhoffer's Crossover
Wire and Tie**

Two single-wire strands with two-point wire barb. Barb holds crossing strands in place. Patented [302422] July 22, 1884, by John W. Nadelhoffer of Joliet, Ill.

Two-point Wire Barbs: *Crossover*

**400
Kittleson's Half Hitch,
Double Strand**

Two-strand wire with two-point wire barb. Barb is tied to one strand with half hitch. Patented [203349] May 7, 1878, by Ole O. Kittleson of Milan, Ill.

Beers–Eaton's Crossover   401

Two-strand wire with two-point wire barb. Barb is a product of machine patented [227948] May 25, 1880, by Edwin A. Beers of De Kalb, and Thomas W. Eaton of Chicago, Ill. Inventor of barb is unknown.

Wiles' Half Hitches   402

Two-strand wire with two-point wire barb. Barb ties in half hitch around each strand. Patented [260268] June 27, 1882, by Robert H. Wiles of Freeport, Ill.

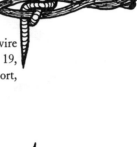

403
Brainerd's Figure Eight
Two-strand wire with two-point wire barb. Patented [264436] September 19, 1882, by Frank W. Brainerd of Freeport, Ill.

404
Brainerd's Figure Eight, Strand Tie Variation
Two-strand wire with two-point wire barb. Variation of patent 264436.

405
Pattison's Cross and Wrap
Two-strand wire with two-point wire barb. Body of barb and one strand are wrapped with one end of the barb. Patented [323724] August 4, 1885, by George H. Pattison of Freeport, Ill.

Two-point Wire Barbs: *Shock Absorber*

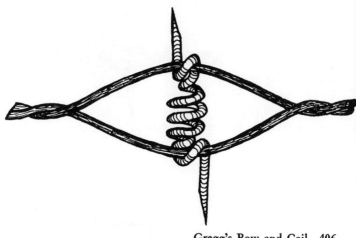

Gregg's Bow and Coil   406
Two-strand wire with two-point wire coil barb. Patented [221300] November 4, 1879, by Samuel H. Gregg of Crawfordsville, Ind.

Butler's Shock Absorber   407
Two-strand wire with two-point, double-coil barb. Barb gives way under load. Patented [248999] November 1, 1881, by William W. Butler of Boise City, Idaho.

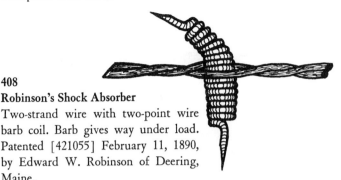

408
Robinson's Shock Absorber
Two-strand wire with two-point wire
barb coil. Barb gives way under load.
Patented [421055] February 11, 1890,
by Edward W. Robinson of Deering,
Maine.

Two-point Wire Barbs: *Pin*

409 Handmade Slit Wire
Single-strand wire slit with chisel to receive two-point wire
barb inserts.

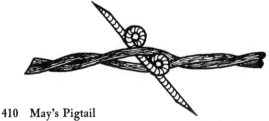

410 May's Pigtail
Two-strand wire with two-point wire barb. Loops prevent
barbs from dropping out. Patented [264728] September 19,
1882, by John M. May of Cedar Rapids, Iowa.

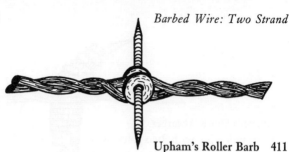

Upham's Roller Barb   411

Two-strand wire with spool and two-point wire barb. Grooved spool with inserted wire barb is gripped between the strands. Patented [286507] October 9, 1883, by Andrew J. Upham of Sterling, Ill.

Upham's Bowed Pin   412

Two-strand wire with two-point wire barb. Half hitches in strands grip barb to prevent end movement. Patented [313391] March 3, 1885, by Andrew J. Upham of Sterling, Ill.

Edenborn's Offset Barb   413

Twisted web wire with two-point wire barb. Barb passes through the thin web. Patented [313929] March 17, 1885, by William Edenborn of St. Louis, Mo.

414   Matteson's Cross-tie

Two-strand wire with two-point wire barb. Bend in body of barb is gripped by loops in strands. Patented [330993] November 24, 1885, by Eugene R. Matteson of Joliet, Ill.

Two-point Wire Barbs: *Strand Clutched*

415   Middleton's Twist

Two-strand wire with two-point twisted wire barb. Barb is shown with a Wire Holder patented [198140] December 11, 1877, by William A. Middleton of Harrisburg, Pa.

416   Beerbower's Two Point

Two-strand wire with two-point wire barb. Barb is flattened across center to receive wire strands. Patented [327755] October 6, 1885, by George Marshall Beerbower of Cherry Vale, Kans.

Blake's Knee Grip 417

Two-strand wire with two-point wire barb. Flattened surfaces in bend of barb are gripped by strands to hold barb in
position. Patented [446607] February 17, 1891, by John W.
Blake of Marshall, Minn.

Curtis' Offset 418

Two twisted half-round wire strands with two-point sheet
metal barb. Barb is gripped between the flat surfaces of the
strands. Patented [514672] February 13, 1894, by John D.
Curtis of Worcester, Mass.

Curtis' Offset, Flattened Strand Variation 419

Flattened two-strand wire with two-point, flat-wire barb.
Tightly twisted strands hold the barb in place. Variation of
patent 514672.

Two-point Wire Barbs: *Integrated Strand*

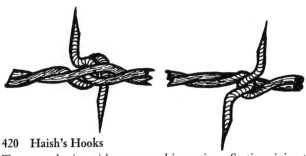

420   Haish's Hooks
Two-strand wire with one strand in sections. Sections join at
ends to form two-point barbs. Patented [146671] January 20,
1874, by Jacob Haish of De Kalb, Ill.

421   Bronson's Link, Double Strand
Staggered wire sections are twisted and joined to form two-
point barbs and continuous fencing. Patented [189994] April
24, 1877, by Adelbert E. Bronson of Chicago, Ill.

422   Washburn's Seated Barb, Double Strand
Two-strand wire with one strand composed of wire sections
joined at ends to form two-point barb. Patented [249212]
November 8, 1881, by Charles F. Washburn of Worcester,
Mass.

Two-point Wire Barbs: *Block and Nail*

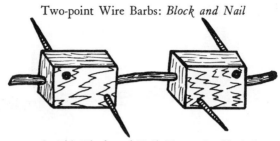

Smith's Block and Nail, Two-point Variation   423
Single-strand wire with two-point, block-and-nail barbs. Wire
strand passes through hole in each block. Variation of patent
66182.

Scutt's Visible Barbed Blocks   424
Two-strand wire with barbed wooden blocks. Lettered blocks
appear at regular intervals in fencing. Patented [224482]
February 10, 1880, by Hiram B. Scutt of Joliet, Ill.

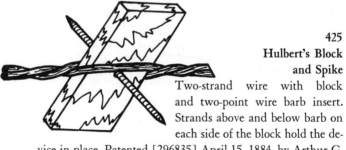

425
**Hulbert's Block
and Spike**
Two-strand wire with block
and two-point wire barb insert.
Strands above and below barb on
each side of the block hold the de-
vice in place. Patented [296835] April 15, 1884, by Arthur G.
Hulbert of St. Louis, Mo.

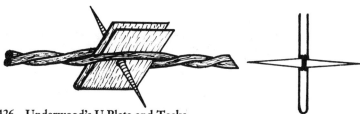

426 Underwood's U-Plate and Tacks

Two-strand wire with metallic block and double-tack barb.
Strands above and below tacks on each side of the block hold
the device in place. Patented [297203] April 22, 1884, by
Henry M. Underwood of Kenosha, Wis.

Two-point Wire Barbs: *Welded*

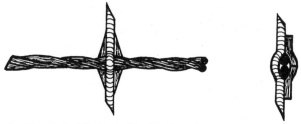

427 Perry's Saddle Barb, Double Strand

Two-strand wire with wire-and-plate barb. Barb and plate
are mounted on both strands and electrically welded. Patented
[588774] August 24, 1897, by John C. Perry of Joliet, Ill.

428 Perry's Cross Stick, Double Strand

Two-strand wire with two-point wire barbs. Barbs are electrically welded to one strand. Patented [588774] August 24,
1897, by John C. Perry of Joliet, Ill.

Perry's Cross Stick, Odd Strands 429

Large and small strands with two-point wire barbs. Barbs are electrically welded to small strand. Patented [588774] August 24, 1897, by John C. Perry of Joliet, Ill.

Three-point Wire Barbs: *Split Point*

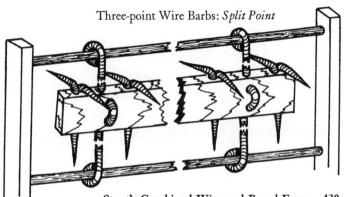

Stout's Combined Wire and Board Fence 430

Single-wire strands at top and bottom of fence support a single board armed with wire spikes. Patented [163116] May 11, 1875, by Stephen Stout of Tremont, Ill.

Edenborn's Webbed Barb 431

Two-strand wire with one-piece, three-point wire barb. Barb ribs are joined at one end by web. Patented [299763] June 3, 1884, by William Edenborn of St. Louis, Mo.

Four-point Wire Barbs: *Coil*

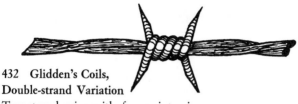

**432 Glidden's Coils,
Double-strand Variation**
Two-strand wire with four-point wire
barb. Barb coils around both strands.
Variation of reissue patent 6914.

**433 Glidden's Coils,
Four-wrap Variation**
Two-strand wire with four-point wire
barb. Barb wraps around both strands.
Variation of reissue patent 6914.

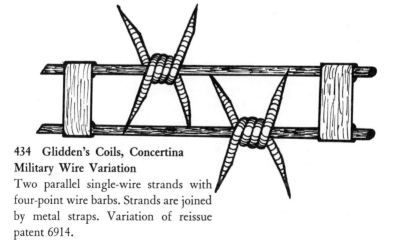

**434 Glidden's Coils, Concertina
Military Wire Variation**
Two parallel single-wire strands with
four-point wire barbs. Strands are joined
by metal straps. Variation of reissue
patent 6914.

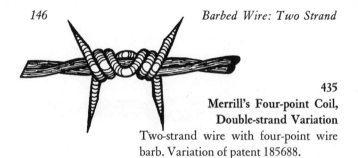

435
**Merrill's Four-point Coil,
Double-strand Variation**
Two-strand wire with four-point wire
barb. Variation of patent 185688.

436
Wager's Coil and Bent Wire
Two-strand wire with loose-fitting, four-
point coil and bent-wire barb. Bent wire
and one strand passed through coil.
Patented [214211] April 8, 1879, by
William H. Wager of Genoa, Ill.

437
Dodge–Washburn's Barb
Two-strand wire with four-point wire
barb. Barb is double wrapped around
one strand. Patented [252746] January
24, 1882, by Thomas H. Dodge and
Charles G. Washburn of Worcester,
Mass.

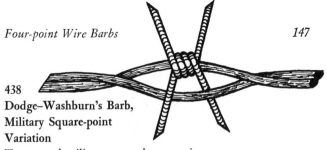

438
Dodge–Washburn's Barb,
Military Square-point
Variation
Two-strand military entanglement wire
with four-point wire barb. Variation of
patent 252746.

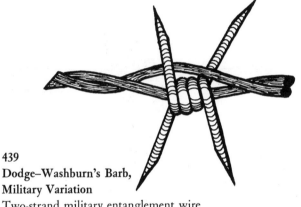

439
Dodge–Washburn's Barb,
Military Variation
Two-strand military entanglement wire
with four-point wire barb. Variation of
patent 252746.

440
Dodge–Washburn's Barb,
Three-wrap Variation
Two-strand wire with four-point wire
barb. Variation of patent 252746.

441

Dodge–Washburn's Barb, Three-wrap Half-round Variation
Two-strand wire with four-point, half-round wire barb. Variation of patent 252746.

442

Edenborn's Double-straddle Barb
Twisted web wire with four-point wire barb. Barb passes through the thin web. Patented [313929] March 17, 1885, by William Edenborn of St. Louis, Mo.

443

Edenborn's Double-straddle Barb, Double-strand Variation
Two-strand wire with four-point wire barb. Variation of patent 313929.

444 Rodden's Webbed Barb
Two-strand wire with half-round, four-point webbed wire barb. Patented [379729] March 20, 1888, by William H. Rodden of Toronto, Can.

445 Curtis' Point Lock
Two-strand wire with four-point, half-round wire barb. Crossing points hold barb parts in place. Patented [494325] March 28, 1893, by John D. Curtis of Worcester, Mass.

446 Curtis' Point Lock, Overlap Variation
Two-strand wire with thin, half-round, four-point barb. Wraps in barb overlap. Variation of patent 494325.

Guilleaume's Fencing Wire   447

Two-strand, diamond-shaped fencing wire for commonly
used wire barbs. Strands lay side by side in twist. Patented
[496974] May 9, 1893, by Theodore Guilleaume of Cologne,
Ger.

Four-point Wire Barbs: *Wrap*

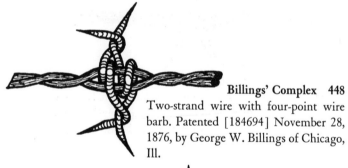

Billings' Complex   448
Two-strand wire with four-point wire
barb. Patented [184694] November 28,
1876, by George W. Billings of Chicago,
Ill.

Burnell's Barb   449

Two-strand wire with four-point wire barb. Patented [192225]
June 19, 1877, by Arthur S. Burnell of Marshalltown, Iowa.

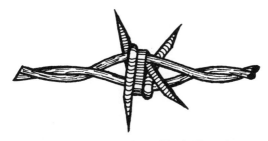

450 Burnell's Barb, Flat–Round-barb Variation
Two-strand wire with four-point wire barb. One part of the two-piece barb is formed from flat wire. Variation of patent 192225.

451 Burnell's Barb, Flat Variation
Two-strand wire with four-point, flat-wire barb. Variation of patent 192225.

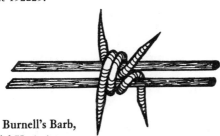

452 Burnell's Barb, Parallel Variation
Two parallel wire strands with four-point wire barb. Variation of patent 192225.

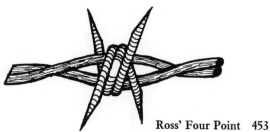

Ross' Four Point   453

Two-strand wire with four-point wire barb. Patented [216294]
June 10, 1879, by Noble G. Ross of Chicago, Ill.

Ross' Four Point, Parallel-strand Variation   454

Two parallel single-wire strands with four-point wire barb.
Variation of patent 216294.

Ross' Four Point, Modern Copper Barb Variation   455

Two-strand wire with four-point copper wire barb. Variation
of patent 216294.

**456 Ross' Barb, Modern
Quarter-flat Variation**
Two-strand high tensile strength wire with quarter-round,
four-point wire barb. Variation of patent 216294.

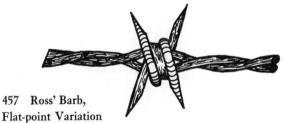

**457 Ross' Barb,
Flat-point Variation**
Two-strand wire with four-point wire barb. Barb consists of
pieces of round and flat wire. Variation of patent 216294.

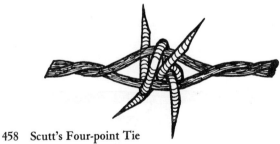

458 Scutt's Four-point Tie
Two-strand wire with four-point wire barb. Patented
[232372] September 21, 1880, by Hiram B. Scutt of Joliet, Ill.

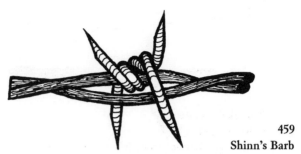

459
Shinn's Barb

Two-strand wire with four-point wire barb. Patented [238447] March 1, 1881, by Milton C. Shinn of Burlington, Iowa.

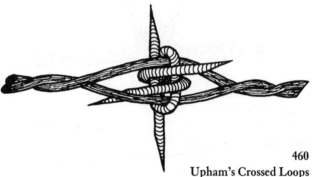

460
Upham's Crossed Loops

Two-strand wire with four-point wire barb. Patented [244953] July 26, 1881, by Andrew J. Upham of Sterling, Ill.

Hill's Caged Barb   461

Two-strand wire with four-point wire barb. Patented [250070] November 29, 1881, by Peter P. Hill of Lee Station, Ill.

462 Decker's Wire and Plate

Two-strand wire with combination wire and sheet metal four-point barb. Patented [254539] March 7, 1882, by Alexander C. Decker of Bushnell, Ill.

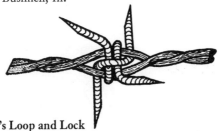

463 Upham's Loop and Lock

Two-strand wire with four-point wire barb. One part of barb loops around both strands and is locked in place by the other. Patented [261185] July 18, 1882, by Andrew J. Upham of Sterling, Ill.

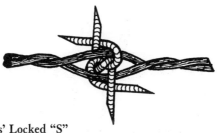

464 Briggs' Locked "S"

Two-strand wire with four-point wire barb. Barb parts interlock with each other and both strands. Patented [272407] February 20, 1883, by Orlando P. Briggs of Chicago, Ill.

Gunderson's Trapped Barb   465

Two-strand wire with four-point wire barb. Points hold barb in position between the strands. Patented [286130] October 2, 1883, by Albert Gunderson of Shabbona, Ill.

Edenborn's Double-straddle Barb, Wrap Variation   466

Two-strand wire with four-point wire barb. Variation of patent 313929.

Curtis' Cross Lock   467

Two-strand wire with half-round, four-point wire barb. Two ends of the barb cross each other between the strands. Patented [494326] March 28, 1893, by John D. Curtis of Worcester, Mass.

468
Curtis' Loop Lock
Two-strand wire with half-round, four-point wire barb.
Patented [494326] March 28, 1893, by John D. Curtis of
Worcester, Mass.

469 Curtis' Cross Lock, Jumbo Hook Variation
Two-strand wire with four-point wire barb. Variation of
patent 494326.

470 Curtis' Cross Lock, Modern Plastic Coat Variation
Two-strand, plastic-coated wire with four-point aluminum
alloy wire barb. Variation of patent 494326.

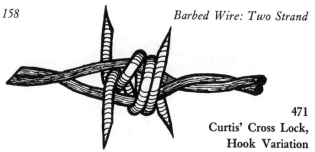

**471
Curtis' Cross Lock,
Hook Variation**

Two-strand wire with four-point wire barb. Variation of patent 494326.

Four-point Wire Barbs: *Twist*

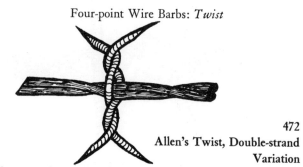

**472
Allen's Twist, Double-strand
Variation**

Two-strand wire with four-point barb. Pieces of wire on each side of the double strands are twisted together to form barb. Variation of patent 180185.

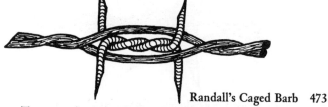

Randall's Caged Barb   473

Two-strand wire with four-point twisted wire barb. Twist in strands traps and holds barb in place. Patented [197172] November 13, 1877, by Frank C. Randall of Joliet, Ill.

474 McFarland's Caged Barb
Two-strand wire with four-point twisted wire barb. Twist in strands traps and holds barb in place. Patented [198135] December 11, 1877, by Lewis H. McFarland of Marshalltown, Iowa.

475 Washburn's Twist
Single-strand wire. Wire is folded, twisted around strand, and cut to form four-point barbs. Patented [200494] February 19, 1878, by Charles F. Washburn of Worcester, Mass.

476 Lenox's Twist
Two-strand wire with four-point wire barb. Barb locks around each strand. Patented [272563] February 20, 1883, by Edwin S. Lenox of Worcester, Mass.

Four-point Wire Barbs: *Kink Locked*

Winterbotham's Caged Barb   477

Two-strand wire with four-point wire barb. Strands make
right angle turns to trap barb. Patented [212080] February 4,
1879, by Joseph Winterbotham of Joliet, Ill.

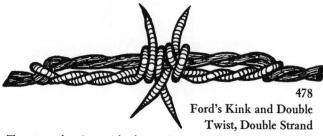

478
Ford's Kink and Double
Twist, Double Strand

Two-strand wire with four-point wire barb. Strands are
kinked to receive twisted barb. Patented [311740] February
3, 1885, by Franklin D. Ford of Providence, R.I.

Four-point Wire Barbs: *Loop Locked*

479
Duncan's Triple Tie, Double Strand
Two-strand wire with one strand looped
to receive interlocking four-point wire
barb. Patented [218506] August 12,
1879, by John A. Duncan of Kansas
City, Mo.

Four-point Wire Barbs: *Staple*

**480   Jayne–Hill's Barb,
Double-strand Wrap Variation**
Two-strand wire with four-point wire barb. Barb is mounted
around both strands. Variation of patent 176120.

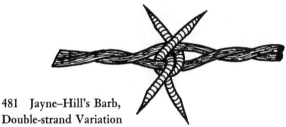

**481   Jayne–Hill's Barb,
Double-strand Variation**
Two-strand wire with two-point wire barb. Barb is mounted
on one strand. Variation of patent 176120.

482   Scutt's Locked Rings
Two-strand wire with four-point wire barb. Patented [195239]
September 18, 1877, by Hiram B. Scutt of Joliet, Ill.

St. John's Locked Staples, Double Strand   483

Two-strand wire with four-point wire barb. Patented [199330]
January 15, 1878, by Spencer H. St. John of Cedar Rapids,
Iowa.

Wing's Two Staple, Double-strand Variation   484

Two-strand wire with four-point wire barb. Variation of
patent 200783.

Billings' Simple   485

Two-strand wire with four-point wire barb. Patented [205234]
June 25, 1878, by Frank Billings of Cleveland, Ohio.

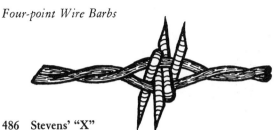

486 Stevens' "X"

Two-strand wire with four-point wire barb. Each half of the barb loops around one strand and straddles the other. Patented [222747] December 16, 1879, by Sidney M. Stevens of De Kalb, Ill.

487 Upham's Loop and Lock, Single-bend Variation

Two-strand wire with four-point wire barb. Variation of patent 261185.

488 Bodman's Matched Loops

Two-strand wire with four-point wire barb. Patented [262200] August 8, 1882, by Charles G. Bodman of De Kalb, Ill.

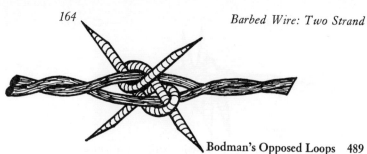

Bodman's Opposed Loops   489

Two-strand wire with four-point wire barb. Patented [262200]
August 8, 1882, by Charles G. Bodman of De Kalb, Ill.

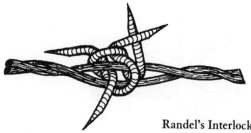

Randel's Interlocking Staples   490

Two-strand wire with four-point interlocking wire barb.
Patented [267253] November 7, 1882, by Charles D. Randel of
New York, N.Y.

Four-point Wire Barbs: *Spreader*

Ellwood's Parallel and Tied Twist   491

Two parallel single-wire strands with
four-point wire barb. Patented [253022]
January 31, 1882, by Abram Ellwood of
Sycamore, Ill.

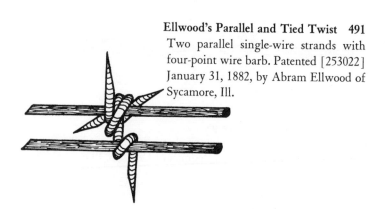

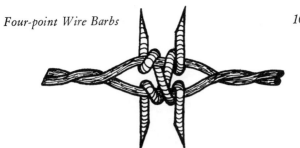

492   Edenborn–Greische's Cross Barbs

Two-strand wire with four-point wire barb. Crossing barb parts are wrapped around each of the two strands. Patented [271693] February 6, 1883, by William Edenborn and Gustav Greische of St. Louis, Mo.

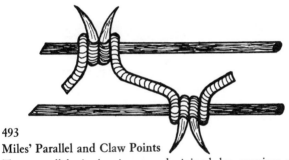

493
Miles' Parallel and Claw Points

Two parallel single-wire strands joined by crossing wire sections with flat, claw-like barb points. Patented [277917] May 22, 1883, by Purches Miles of Brooklyn, N.Y.

494   Root's Locked Arms

Two-strand wire with two-point inter-locking wire barb. Patented [281300] July 17, 1883, by William A. Root of New York, N.Y.

Four-point Wire Barbs: *Split Wire*

Lord's Split Wire   495

Two-strand wire with four-point wire barb. Barbs are made of wire sections split at right angles. Patented [293584] February 12, 1884, by Tyler C. Lord of Joliet, Ill.

Curtis' Split Half Round   496

Two-strand wire with four-point, half-round wire barb. Patented [484890] October 25, 1892, by John D. Curtis of Worcester, Mass.

Four-point Wire Barbs: *Plate Locked*

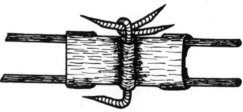

Mouck's Three-to-one Barb, Parallel Strand   497

Two parallel single-wire strands with four-point wire barb. Barb is held in place with clip-on sheet metal plate. Patented [507088] October 17, 1893, by Solomon F. Mouck of Denver, Colo.

Multi-point Wire Barbs: *Wire Rowel*

498 Hodge's Wire Rowel
Twisted wire strands spread at regular intervals to receive six-point wire barbs. Barb rotates on a wire serving both as shaft and spreader. Patented [392433] November 6, 1888, by Chester A. Hodge of Chicago, Ill.

One-point Sheet Metal Barbs: *Leaf*

499 Delffs' Leaf
Two-strand wire with leaf-shaped sheet metal barb. Barbs make fencing visible. Patented [490187] January 17, 1893, by Arnold Delffs of Bedford, Tenn.

Two-point Sheet Metal Barbs: *Wrap*

500 Brotherton's Barb, Flat Variation
Two-strand wire with two-point, flat-wire barb. Variation of patent 207710.

Brink's Notched Plate, Double Strand   501

Two-strand wire with two-point sheet metal barb. Patented [258014] May 16, 1882, by Jacob and Warren M. Brinkerhoff of Auburn, N.Y.

Brink's Butt Plate, Double Strand   502

Two-strand wire with two-point sheet metal barb. Patented [258014] May 16, 1882, by Jacob and Warren H. Brinkerhoff of Auburn, N.Y.

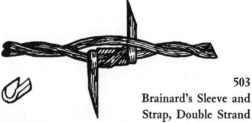

503
Brainard's Sleeve and Strap, Double Strand

Two-strand wire with sheet metal sleeve and two-point barb. Sleeve is crimped to one strand to hold barb in place. Patented [298440] May 13, 1884, by Curtis B. Brainard of Joliet, Ill.

504 Nadelhoffer's Flat-wire Gull Wing
Two-strand wire with flat-wire, two-point barb. Patented
[307673] November 4, 1884, by John W. Nadelhoffer of
Joliet, Ill.

Two-point Sheet Metal Barbs: *Perforated*

505 Kelly's Thorny Fence, Double Strand
Two-strand wire with curved two-point, diamond-shaped
sheet metal barb. Patented [74379] February 11, 1868, by
Michael Kelly of New York, N.Y.

506 Kelly's Thorny Fence, Common Variation
Two-strand wire with two-point, diamond-shaped sheet metal
barb. Variation of patent 74379.

Kelly's Thorny Fence, Mixed-barb Variation   507

Two-strand wire with two-point, alternating sheet metal and
wire barbs. Variation of patent 74379.

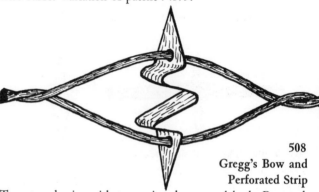

508
Gregg's Bow and
Perforated Strip

Two-strand wire with two-point sheet metal barb. Patented
[221300] November 4, 1879, by Samuel H. Gregg of Crawfordsville, Ind.

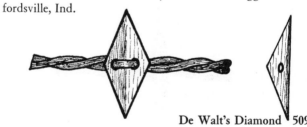

De Walt's Diamond   509

Two-strand wire with two-point sheet metal barb. Barb is
perforated and slightly folded to receive one strand. Patented
[312440] February 17, 1885, by George De Walt of Kenton,
Ohio.

Two-point Sheet Metal Barbs: *Clip*

510 Upham's Diamond with Anchor Lugs
Two-strand wire with two-point sheet metal barb. Lugs grip
the strands to hold barb in place. Patented [301186] July 1,
1884, by Andrew J. Upham of Sterling, Ill.

511 Scutt's Crimp Barb,
Flat-wire Variation
Two-strand wire with two-point, flat-wire barb. Bent body
holds barb in place. Variation of patent 332755.

Two-point Sheet Metal Barbs: *Strand Clutched*

512 Armstrong–Doolittle's Notched Diamond
Two-strand wire with two-point sheet
metal barb. Notches and tight twist in
wire strands hold barb in place. Patented
[168550] October 11, 1875, by Frank
Armstrong and George Doolittle of
Bridgeport, Conn.

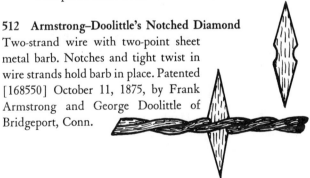

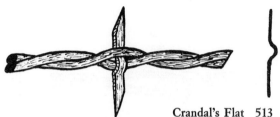

Crandal's Flat   513

Two-strand wire with two-point sheet metal barb. Patented
[247540] September 27, 1881, by Edward M. Crandal of
Chicago, Ill.

Crandal's Flat Offset   514

Two-strand wire with two-point sheet metal barb. Patented
[247540] September 27, 1881, by Edward M. Crandal of
Chicago, Ill.

Haish's Grooved Wire and Barb   515

Two-strand grooved wire with grooved, two-point sheet metal
barb. Grooves in wire hold barb in place. Patented [261704]
July 25, 1882, by Jacob Haish of De Kalb, Ill.

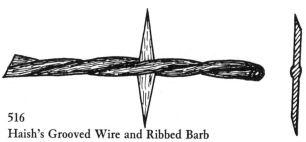

516
Haish's Grooved Wire and Ribbed Barb
Two-strand grooved wire with two-point, ribbed sheet metal barb. Barb is held in place by groove and rib. Patented [261704] July 25, 1882, by Jacob Haish of De Kalb, Ill.

517
Upham's Screw Barb
Two-strand wire with two-point sheet metal barb. Barb is cut from pretwisted stock. Patented [294827] March 11, 1884, by Andrew J. Upham of Sterling, Ill.

518
Griswold's Ribbed Barb
Two-strand wire with ribbed sheet metal barb. Barb is cross slit with short fins bent at right angles to long fins. Rib dent and short fins hold barb in place. Patented [377252] January 31, 1888, by J. Wool Griswold of Troy, N.Y.

Griswold's Center-core Barb 519

Two-strand wire with center-core sheet metal barb. Barb is cross-slit with short fins bent at right angles to long fins. Dents in core and short fins hold barb in place. Patented [377252] January 31, 1888, by J. Wool Griswold of Troy, N.Y.

Griswold's Fastener 520

Two-strand wire with two-point sheet metal barb. Folded barb strip with points spread is anchored between the wire strands. Patented [380388] April 3, 1888, by J. Wool Griswold of Troy, N.Y.

Two-point Sheet Metal Barbs: *Square Plate*

521
Barr's Two-point Barb Plate

Two-strand wire with two-point sheet metal barb plate. Notches cut in edges hold plate in position. Patented [289207] November 27, 1883, by Charles H. Barr of Pittsburgh, Pa.

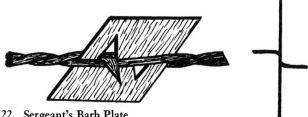

522 Sergeant's Barb Plate
Two-strand wire with two-point sheet metal barb plate. Barb points bend in opposite directions to hold plate in place. Patented [299169] May 27, 1884, by Raphael Sergeant of Pittsburgh, Pa.

Two-point Sheet Metal Barbs: *Fence Strap*

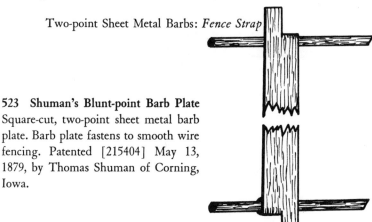

523 Shuman's Blunt-point Barb Plate
Square-cut, two-point sheet metal barb plate. Barb plate fastens to smooth wire fencing. Patented [215404] May 13, 1879, by Thomas Shuman of Corning, Iowa.

Two-point Malleable and Cast Iron Barbs: *Clip*

**524 Stover's Barb,
Corsicana Clip Variation**
Two-strand wire with two-point cast barb. Variation of patent 164947.

Haish's Anvil Barb   525
Two-strand wire with two-point, crimped-on iron barb. Patented [332252] December 15, 1885, by Jacob Haish of De Kalb, Ill.

Haish's Horn Barb   526
Two-strand wire with two-point, crimped-on iron barb. Patented [332252] December 15, 1885, by Jacob Haish of De Kalb, Ill.

Two-point Malleable and Cast Iron Barbs: *Pin*

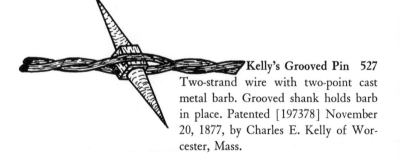

Kelly's Grooved Pin   527
Two-strand wire with two-point cast metal barb. Grooved shank holds barb in place. Patented [197378] November 20, 1877, by Charles E. Kelly of Worcester, Mass.

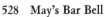

528   May's Bar Bell
Two-strand wire with two-point cast iron barb. Ring barriers prevent barb dropping out. Patented [264728] September 19, 1882, by John M. May of Cedar Rapids, Iowa.

529   Dodge's Knobby Barb
Two-strand wire with two-point metal barb. Knobs are pressed in surface of barb to receive wire strands and to keep barb from turning. Patented [289076] November 27, 1883, by Thomas H. Dodge of Worcester, Mass.

Three-point Sheet Metal Barbs: *Wrap*

530   Brink's Three-point Long Plate
Two-strand wire with three-point sheet metal barb. One point wraps around one strand to hold barb in place. Patented [258706] May 30, 1882, by Jacob and Warren M. Brinkerhoff of Auburn, N.Y.

Brink's Stinger   531

Two-strand wire with three-point sheet metal barb. Patented [269631] December 26, 1882, by John J. Brinkerhoff of Auburn, N.Y.

Three-point Sheet Metal Barbs: *Rider*

Pooler–Jones' Barb, Double-strand Variation   532

Two-strand wire with three-point sheet metal barb. Variation of patent 181537.

Three-point Sheet Metal Barbs: *Strand Clutched*

Armstrong's Arrow Point   533

Two-strand wire with three-point sheet metal barb. Patented [171208] December 31, 1875, by Frank Armstrong of Bridgeport, Conn.

534 Armstrong's Arrow Point, Double Strand

Double-strand wire with three-point sheet metal barb. Barb
is held in place by two lugs and two points. Patented [182626]
September 24, 1876, by Frank Armstrong of Bridgeport,
Conn.

535 Havenhill's Arrow Point

Two-strand wire with three-point sheet metal barb. Patented
[205639] July 2, 1878, by Edwin Havenhill of Joliet, Ill.

Four-point Sheet Metal Barbs: *Wrap*

**536
Brink's Balanced
Diamond**

Two-strand wire with four-point sheet metal barb. Outer lugs
are wrapped around one strand locking barb in position.
Patented [267485] November 14, 1882, by John J. Brinkerhoff
of Auburn, N.Y.

Brink's Balanced Strip   537

Two-strand wire with four-point sheet metal barb. Outer strip and lug are wrapped around one strand locking barb in position. Patented [267485] November 14, 1882, by John J. Brinkerhoff of Auburn, N.Y.

Brink's Curb   538

Two-strand wire with four-point sheet metal barb. Patented [269631] December 26, 1882, by John J. Brinkerhoff of Auburn, N.Y.

Brink's Burr   539

Two-strand wire with four-point sheet metal barb. Patented [269631] December 26, 1882, by John J. Brinkerhoff of Auburn, N.Y.

540 Brink's Saddle

Two-strand wire with four-point sheet metal barb. Patented [269631] December 26, 1882, by John J. Brinkerhoff of Auburn, N.Y.

541 Brink's Cradle

Two-strand wire with four-point sheet metal barb. Patented [269631] December 26, 1882, by John J. Brinkerhoff of Auburn, N.Y.

Four-point Sheet Metal Barbs: *Clip*

542 Scutt's Double Clip, Double Strand

Two-strand wire with four-point sheet metal barb. Offset cuts in metal plate allow barb points to project at right angles to each other. Patented [193557] July 24, 1877, by Hiram B. Scutt of Joliet, Ill.

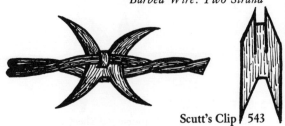

Scutt's Clip 543

Two-strand wire with four-point sheet metal barb. Clip grips
one strand. Patented [205000] June 18, 1878, by Hiram B.
Scutt of Joliet, Ill.

Gregg's Bow and Split Strip 544

Two-strand wire with four-point sheet metal barb. Patented
[221300] November 4, 1879, by Samuel H. Gregg of Crawfordsville, Ind.

Baker's Locked Clips 545

Two-strand wire with four-point, ring-locked sheet metal
barb. Patented [233832] November 2, 1880, by George C.
Baker of Des Moines, Iowa.

Four-point Sheet Metal Barbs: *Joint Locked*

546   Brown–Tubbs' Joined Triangles

Two-strand wire with four-point sheet metal barb. Patented [170518] November 30, 1875, by Warren L. Brown and Lawrence G. Tubbs of Dunlap, Iowa.

547   Burrows' Joined Diamonds

Two-strand wire with four-point sheet metal barb. Barb parts are friction locked. Patented [192736] July 3, 1877, by William T. Burrows of Nashua, Iowa.

Four-point Sheet Metal Barbs: *Spinner*

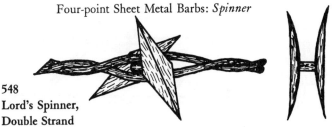

548
Lord's Spinner,
Double Strand

Two-strand wire with four-point sheet metal barb. Diamond-shaped barb plates are joined by a shaft and rotate under load. Patented [218290] August 5, 1879, by Tylor C. Lord of Joliet, Ill.

Lord's Spinner Plate   549

Two-strand wire with four-point sheet metal barb. Shaft formed from central tongues allows barb to rotate under load. Patented [218290] August 5, 1879, by Tylor C. Lord of Joliet, Ill.

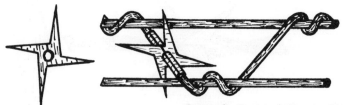

Guenzel's Star and Sleeve   550

Two parallel single-wire strands with four-point sheet metal barb. Barb and sleeve are mounted on diagonal cross wire. Patented [452002] May 12, 1891, by Edward B. Guenzel of Tracy, Iowa.

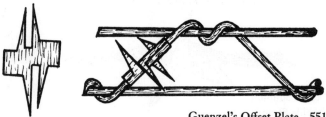

Guenzel's Offset Plate   551

Two parallel single-wire strands with four-point sheet metal barb plate. Barb plate is mounted on diagonal cross wire. Patented [452002] May 12, 1891, by Edward B. Guenzel of Tracy, Iowa.

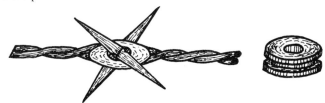

552   Funcheon's Spool and Spinner
Two-strand wire with four-point sheet metal barb. Barb rotates in hole through grooved metal spool gripped between the strands. Patented [493210] March 7, 1893, by Daniel C. Funcheon of Valverde, Colo.

Four-point Sheet Metal Barbs: *Square Plate*

553   Havenhill's "N" Plate
Two-strand wire with four-point sheet metal barb. Barb is notched to receive strands. Patented [205639] July 2, 1878, by Edwin Havenhill of Joliet, Ill.

**554
Parker's Caged
Plate**
Two-strand wire with four-point sheet metal barb. Barb is trapped by twist in strands. Patented [211863] February 4, 1879, by Charles P. Parker of Joliet, Ill.

Shuman's Blunt Four Point   555

Two-strand wire with square-cut, four-point sheet metal barb. Patented [215404] May 13, 1879, by Thomas Shuman of Corning, Iowa.

Scutt's Plate, Handmade Variation   556
Two-strand wire with four-point sheet metal barb. Variation of patent 215404.

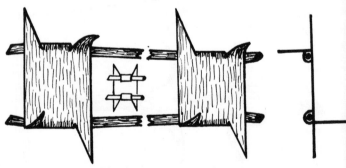

Elsey's Varying Strands, Side-cut Barb   557

Two single-wire strands with four-point sheet metal barb plates. Distance between strands varies with alternate barbs.

Patented [261212] July 18, 1882, by George Elsey of Springfield, Mass.

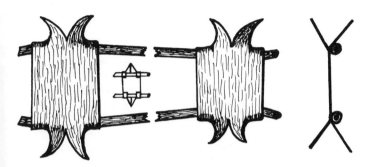

558 Elsey's Varying Strands, Center-cut Barb
Two single-wire strands with four-point sheet metal barb plates. Distance between strands varies with alternate barbs. Patented [261212] July 18, 1882, by George Elsey of Springfield, Mass.

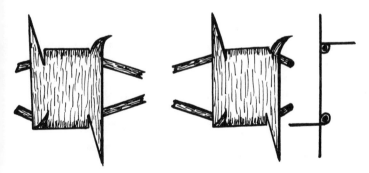

559 Elsey's Crossing Strands
Two single-wire strands with four-point sheet metal barb plate. Strands cross between plates. Patented [261212] July 18, 1882, by George Elsey of Springfield, Mass.

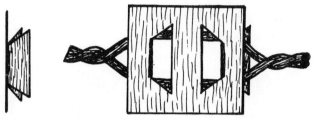

Ford's Square Plate   560

Two-strand wire with four-point sheet metal barb plate. Lugs are punched from center of plate to receive strands. Patented [287372] October 23, 1883, by John C. Ford of Pittsburgh, Pa.

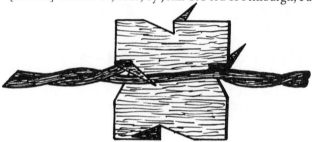

Barr's Side-cut Barb Plate   561

Two-strand wire with four-point metal barb plate. Notches cut in edges hold plate in position. Patented [289207] November 27, 1883, by Charles H. Barr of Pittsburgh, Pa.

Four-point Sheet Metal Barbs: *"H" Plate*

Scutt's Plate, Thick-center "H" Variation   562

Two-strand wire with four-point sheet metal barb. Body of

barb tapers outward from center toward the points. Variation of patent 180656.

563 Scutt's Plate, "H" Variation
Two-strand wire with four-point sheet metal barb. Variation of patent 180656.

564 Watkins' Barb, H-plate Variation
Two-strand wire with four-point sheet metal barb. Variation of patent 184486.

565 Swan's "H" Plate
Two-strand wire with four-point sheet metal barb. Patented [216358] June 10, 1879, by Frank Swan of Joliet, Ill.

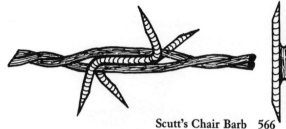

Scutt's Chair Barb 566

Two-strand wire with four-point wire barb. Barb is cut from webbed wire blank. Patented [264110] September 12, 1882, by John F. Scutt of Joliet, Ill.

Four-point Sheet Metal Barbs: *Vee Plate*

Scutt's Vee Plate 567

Two-strand wire with four-point sheet metal barb. Barb is wrapped around the strands in opposite directions with points spread. Patented [180656] August 1, 1876, by Hiram B. Scutt of Joliet, Ill.

Scutt's Plate, Thick-center Variation 568

Two-strand wire with four-point sheet metal barb. Body of

the barb tapers from the center toward the points. Variation of patent 180656.

569   Scutt's Plate, M-over-W Variation
Two-strand wire with four-point sheet metal barb. Lower right and upper left points are cut diagonally. Variation of patent 180656.

570   Watkins' Vee Plate
Two-strand wire with four-point sheet metal barb. Barb is held in position between the strands by spread points. Patented [184486] November 21, 1876, by William Watkins of Joliet, Ill.

571   Hart's Notched Barb
Two-strand wire with notched, four-point sheet metal barb. Barb is held in position by the strands resting in the notches. Patented [312463] February 17, 1885, by Hubert C. Hart of Unionville, Conn.

Hart's Stringer Barb   572

Two-strand wire with perforated, four-point sheet metal barb. Barb is held in place by one strand through the holes. Patented [312463] February 17, 1885, by Hubert C. Hart of Unionville, Conn.

Four-point Sheet Metal Barbs: *Arrow Plate*

Scutt's Plate, Arrow-point Variation   573

Two-strand wire with four-point sheet metal barb. Barb is shaped like an arrowhead. Variation of patent 180656.

574

Scutt's Plate, Leaning Arrow-point Variation

Two-strand wire with four-point sheet metal barb. Barb is

shaped by off-center cuts in metal plate. Variation of patent 180656.

575 Scutt's Plate, Block and Arrow-point Variation
Two-strand wire with alternating blocks and four-point sheet metal barbs. Blocks are notched to receive the wire strands. Variation of patent 180656.

576 Watkins' Barb, Arrow-point Variation
Two-strand wire with four-point sheet metal barb. Variation of patent 184486.

577 Oliver's Ribbed Arrow Point
Two-strand wire with four-point, ribbed sheet metal barb. Patented [286147] October 2, 1883, by James B. Oliver of Pittsburgh, Pa.

Four-point Sheet Metal Barbs: *Diamond Plate*

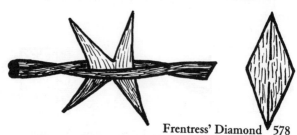

Frentress' Diamond 578

Two-strand wire with diamond-shaped, two-point sheet metal barb. Patented [171008] December 14, 1875, by Henry N. Frentress of Dunleith, Ill.

Watkins' Diamond 579

Two-strand wire with four-point sheet metal barb. Barb is held in position between the strands by spread points. Patented [184486] November 21, 1876, by William Watkins of Joliet, Ill.

Cherry–Wheeler's Double Diamond   580

Two-strand wire with four-point sheet metal barb. Barb is

folded and points spread at right angles. Patented [195091] September 11, 1877, by Hamilton Cherry and Harry E. Wheeler of Aurora, Ill.

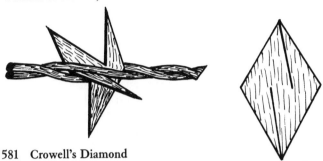

581   Crowell's Diamond
Two-strand wire with four-point sheet metal barb. Patented [215888] May 27, 1879, by John S. Crowell of Springfield, Ohio.

582   Oliver's Ribbed Diamond
Two-strand wire with four-point, ribbed sheet metal barb. Patented [286147] October 2, 1883, by James B. Oliver of Pittsburgh, Pa.

583
Brainard's Vented Diamond
Two-strand wire with two-point sheet metal barb. Punch-out lugs grip strands to hold barb in place. Patented [287091] October 23, 1883, by Curtis B. Brainard of Joliet, Ill.

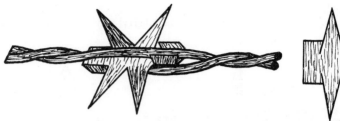

Upham's Double Diamond with Anchor Lugs 584

Two-strand wire with four-point sheet metal barb. Lugs grip strands to hold barb in place. Patented [301186] July 1, 1884, by Andrew J. Upham of Sterling, Ill.

Four-point Sheet Metal Barbs: *Star*

Pond's Square Barb 585

Two-strand wire with four-point sheet metal barb plate. Cuts made in barb permit twisting of one point so that barb may be mounted on the strands. Patented [270116] January 2, 1883, by Orlando M. Pond of Independence, Iowa.

Shellaberger's Star 586

Two-strand wire with four-point, rotating sheet metal barb. Spread in wire strands holds barb in place. Patented [272091] February 13, 1883, by Kirk L. Shellaberger of Dayton, Ohio.

587   Morgan's Star
Two-strand wire with four-point sheet metal barb. Barb is held in place by twist in strands. Patented [302275] July 22, 1884, by Thomas H. Morgan of Pittsburgh, Pa.

Four-point Sheet Metal Barbs: *Fence Strap*

588
Shuman's Four-point Barb
Plate, Side Cut
Barbed sheet metal plate with ends fastened to smooth strands of fence wire. Patented [211349] January 14, 1879, by Thomas Shuman of Corning, Iowa.

589
Shuman's Four-point
Barb Plate
Sheet metal barb plate. Plate is fastened to smooth wire strands in fencing. Patented [238255] March 1, 1881, by Thomas Shuman of Corning, Iowa.

Four-point Malleable and Cast Iron Barbs: *Star*

Reynolds' Cast Barb   590

Two-strand wire with perforated, four-point cast iron barb. Patented [187049] February 6, 1877, by William L. Reynolds of St. Louis, Mo.

Burrows' Star   591

Two-strand wire with four-point cast iron barb. Patented [194647] August 28, 1877, by William T. Burrows of Nashua, Iowa.

Pederson's Star   592

Two-strand wire with four-point, cast or malleable iron barb. Grooves and fin hold barb in place. Patented [205501] July 2, 1878, by Ole Pederson of Joliet, Ill.

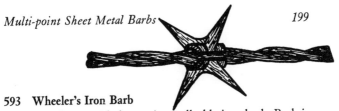

593   Wheeler's Iron Barb

Two-strand wire with four-point malleable iron barb. Barb is clamped to prestretched wire strands. Patented [321264] June 30, 1885, by Alonzo S. Wheeler of Sangutuck, Conn.

Multi-point Sheet Metal Barbs: *Square Plate*

594   Stubbe's Large Formee Cross

Two-strand wire with eight-point sheet metal barb plate. Square plate is cut inward from corners and bent to form barb points. Patented [287337] October 23, 1883, by John Stubbe of Pittsburgh, Pa.

595   Stubbe's Small Formee Cross

Two-strand wire with eight-point sheet metal barb plate. Square plate is cut inward from corners and bent to form barb points. Patented [287337] October 23, 1883, by John Stubbe of Pittsburgh, Pa.

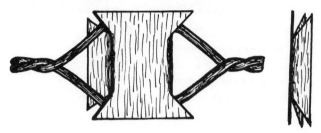

Ford's Corner-cut Barb Plate   596

Two-strand wire with eight-point sheet metal barb plate. Cuts are made in plate corners to receive strands. Patented [287372] October 23, 1883, by John C. Ford of Pittsburgh, Pa.

Barr's Corner-cut Barb Plate   597

Two-strand wire with eight-point sheet metal barb plate. Notches cut in edges hold plate in position. Patented [289207] November 27, 1883, by Charles H. Barr of Pittsburgh, Pa.

598   Forrester's Corner-cut Barb Plate
Two-strand wire with sixteen-point sheet metal barb plate.
Barb plate is cut and bent at right angles to receive strands.
Patented [298193] May 6, 1884, by Samuel Forrester of Alle-
gheny City, Pa.

599   Forrester's Saw-tooth Barb Plate, Vertical Cut
Two-strand wire with twelve-point sheet metal barb plate.
Barb plate is cut and bent at right angles to receive strands.
Patented [298193] May 6, 1884, by Samuel Forrester of Alle-
gheny City, Pa.

Forrester's Saw-tooth Barb Plate, Diagonal Cut   600
Two-strand wire with twelve-point sheet metal barb plate.
Barb plate is cut and bent at right angles to receive strands.
Patented [298193] May 6, 1884, by Samuel Forrester of
Allegheny City, Pa.

Multi-point Sheet Metal Barbs: *Diamond Plate*

Armstrong's Diamond   601
Two-strand wire with five-point sheet metal barb. Two points
of the barb wrap around one strand. Patented [176262] April
18, 1876, by Frank Armstrong of Bridgeport, Conn.

Cherry–Wheeler's Triple Diamond   602
Two-strand wire with six-point sheet metal barb. Barb is

folded and outer points spread at right angles. Patented [195091] September 11, 1877, by Hamilton Cherry and Harry E. Wheeler of Aurora, Ill.

Multi-point Sheet Metal Barbs: *Spreader Plate*

603   Cherry–Wheeler's Triple Diamond, Flat Variation
Two-strand wire with six-point sheet metal barb. Variation of patent 195091.

604   Hart's Spreader
Two-strand wire with slotted, eight-point sheet metal barb. Strands pass through slot and points to hold barb in place. Patented [312463] February 17, 1885, by Hubert C. Hart of Unionville, Conn.

Multi-point Sheet Metal Barbs: *Wheel*

Stoll's Spur Wheel   605

Two-strand wire with twelve-point sheet metal barb. Barb rotates under load. Patented [230445] July 27, 1880, by Jacob Stoll of Fountain City, Wis.

Barker's Spur Wheel, Double Strand   606

Two-strand wire with twelve-point sheet metal barb. Barb rotates on wire shaft fastened to wire strands. Patented [251505] December 27, 1881, by George E. Barker of Waverly, N.Y.

Mihills' Spur Wheel   607

Two-strand wire with grooved plate and free-turning, eight-point sheet metal barb. Patented [269444] December 19, 1882, by Merrick A. Mihills of Painesville, Ohio.

608   Shellaberger's Spur Wheel
Two-strand wire with eight-point, rotating sheet metal barb.
Spread in wire strands holds barb in place. Patented [272091]
February 13, 1883, by Kirk L. Shellaberger of Dayton, Ohio.

609   Hyde's Spur Wheel
Two-strand wire with sheet metal barb having eight staggered points. Barb rotates on iron shaft split at each end to
receive strands. Patented [277288] May 8, 1883, by Charles
F. Hyde of Ottawa, Kans.

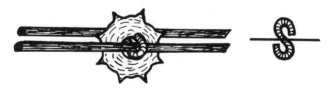

610   Goss' Spur Wheel
Two parallel single-wire strands with eight-point sheet metal
barb. Barb rotates on S-shaped wire shaft. Patented [282453]
July 31, 1883, by Joseph Goss of Beloit, Wis.

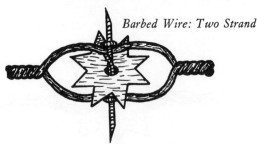

Evans' Spur Wheel, Double Strand   611

Two-strand wire with eight-point sheet metal barb. Strands are parted to cage barb and support pointed shaft and tie wire. Patented [287261] October 23, 1883, by John Elias Evans of Spanish Fork, Utah.

Hodge's Spur Wheel, Parallel Strands   612

Two parallel single-wire strands with fourteen-point sheet metal barb wheel. Barb wheel turns on wire shaft joining the strands. Patented [367398] August 2, 1887, by Chester A. Hodge of Beloit, Wis.

Hodge's Spur Wheel, Twisted Strands   613

Two-strand wire with fourteen-point sheet metal barb wheel. Barb wheel turns on wire shaft joining the strands. Patented [367398] August 2, 1887, by Chester A. Hodge of Beloit, Wis.

614   Hodge's Spur Wheel, Eight-point Variation
Two-strand wire with eight-point sheet metal barb wheel.
Barb wheel turns on wire shaft joining the strands. Variation
of patent 367398.

615   Hodge's Spur Wheel, Ten-point Variation
Two-strand wire with ten-point sheet metal barb wheel. Barb
turns on wire shaft joining the two strands. Variation of
patent 367398.

Multi-point Sheet Metal Barbs: *Star*

616   Stover's Star
Two-strand wire with five-point sheet metal barb. Barb is
mounted between the strands with one point crimped around
a strand. Patented [250014] November 22, 1881, by Daniel C.
Stover of Freeport, Ill.

Multi-point Sheet Metal Barbs: *Zigzag Strip*

Crandal's Zigzag   617

Two-strand wire with interlacing sheet metal barb strip. Patented [221158] November 4, 1879, by Edward M. Crandal of Chicago, Ill.

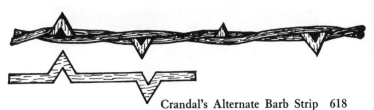

Crandal's Alternate Barb Strip   618

Two-strand wire with continuous sheet metal strip twisted with the strands. Patented [247539] September 27, 1881, by Edward M. Crandal of Chicago, Ill.

Crandal's Vertical Barb Strip   619

Two-strand wire with continuous sheet metal strip twisted with the strands. Patented [247539] September 27, 1881, by Edward M. Crandal of Chicago, Ill.

Multi-point Sheet Metal Barbs: *Fence Strap*

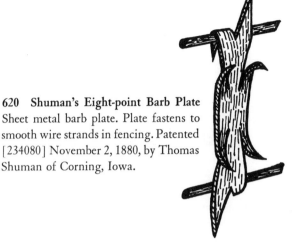

620   Shuman's Eight-point Barb Plate
Sheet metal barb plate. Plate fastens to
smooth wire strands in fencing. Patented
[234080] November 2, 1880, by Thomas
Shuman of Corning, Iowa.

**621   Riter's Double-edge
Saw-tooth Slat**
Sheet metal strip with serrated edges.
Strips are fastened vertically to strands
of wire in fencing. Patented [352428]
November 9, 1886, by John L. Riter of
Brownsville, Ind.

Riter's Single-edge Saw-tooth Slat   622

Sheet metal strips with serrated edge. Twin strips are fastened vertically to strands of wire fencing. Patented [352428] November 9, 1886, by John L. Riter of Brownsville, Ind.

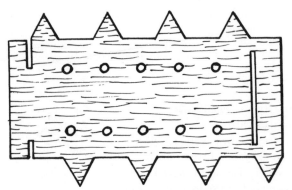

Cloud's Barbed Warning Strip   623

Perforated sheet metal plate with projecting barbs. Plates are joined at slits and wire-tied to form continuous warning strip. Patented [367893] August 9, 1887, by William J. Cloud of Junction City, Tex.

Multi-point Malleable and Cast Iron Barbs: *Wheel*

624   Gearty's Two-piece Spur Wheel
Two-strand wire with eight-point, two-piece barb wheel.
Wheel has an internal groove that rides an S-shaped wire
between the strands. A rivet holds the two parts of the wheel
together. Patented [472044] April 5, 1892, by Hugh Gearty
of Springfield, Ill.

Multi-point Malleable and Cast Iron Barbs: *Bur*

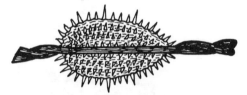

625   Phillips' Solid Cocklebur
Two-strand wire with metallic bur. Channels are placed in
sides of bur to receive the wire strands. Patented [280857]
July 10, 1883, by Oliver O. Phillips of Allegheny, Pa.

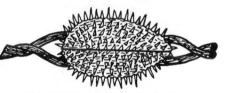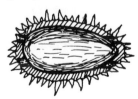

626   Phillips' Hollow Cocklebur
Two-strand wire with metallic bur. Holes are drilled in ends

of bur to receive wire strands. Patented [280857] July 10, 1883, by Oliver O. Phillips of Allegheny, Pa.

Multi-point Malleable and Cast Iron Barbs: *Cylinder*

Utter's Cylinder   627

Two-strand wire with barbed metal tube. Barbed tube moves freely between sheet metal stays gripped by the twisted strands. Patented [369825] September 13, 1887, by Homer Utter of Cuba, N.Y.

Multi-point Malleable and Cast Iron Barbs: *Disc*

Neely–Marland's Disc   628

Two-strand wire with knife-edge, circular sheet metal barb. Patented [251273] December 20, 1881, by Thomas Neely and Alfred Marland of Pittsburgh, Pa.

BARBED WIRE: Three Strand

One-point Barbs: *Tack*

629   Underwood's Tack
Three-strand wire with single-tack barb. Patented [206754]
August 6, 1878, by Henry M. Underwood of Kenosha, Wis.

Two-point Wire Barbs: *Single Turn*

630   Clark's Wire Rail With Outside-wrap Barb
Three parallel single-wire strands with two-point wire barbs.
Barbs alternately pass around two strands and three strands.
Patented [260844] July 11, 1882, by Norman Clark of Sterl-
ing, Ill.

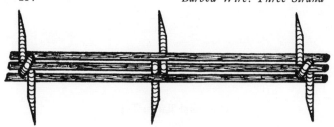

Clark's Wire Rail With Inside-wrap Barb   631

Three parallel single-wire strands with two-point wire barbs. Barbs wrapped around center strand alternating from one side of rail to the other. Patented [260844] July 11, 1882, by Norman Clark of Sterling, Ill.

Baker's Barb, Three Barbed Strand Variation   632

Three-strand wire with two-point, flat-wire barbs. Barbs are mounted on separate strands. Variation of patent 273219.

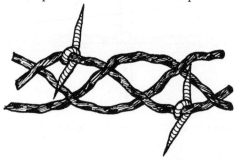

Riter's Corrugated Visible Wire with Barbs   633

Three-strand, braided corrugated fencing with two-point wire barbs. Patented [506257] October 10, 1893, by John L. Riter of Brownsville, Ind.

634 Riter's Visible Lace Wire with Barbs
Parallel undulating single-wire strands with two-point wire barbs. Strands are joined by intertwining smaller wire. Patented [506258] October 10, 1893, by John L. Riter of Brownsville, Ind.

Two-point Wire Barbs: *Coil*

635 Hanging Barb, Three Strand
Three-strand wire with two-point wire barb. Barb wraps around one strand with points extended in the same direction. Inventor of barb is unknown.

636 Glidden's Barb, Three-strand Variation
Three-strand wire with two-point wire barb. Variation of patent 157124.

637
Glidden's Barb,
Light-duty Small and Two
Large-strand Variation

Three-strand wire with two-point wire barb. One strand is of a smaller gauge than the other two. Variation of patent 157124.

638
Glidden's Barb, Small and
Two Large-strand Variation

Three-strand wire with two-point wire barb. One strand is of a smaller gauge than the other two. Variation of patent 157124.

639
Glidden's Barb, Half Round
in Three-strand Variation

Three-strand wire with two-point wire barb. Two strands are round and one half round. Variation of patent 157124.

640
Glidden's Barb, Wrapped
Three-strand Variation

Three-strand wire with two-point wire barb. Barb wraps around the three strands. Variation of patent 157124.

641 Glidden's Barb, Paired Barbs Three-strand Variation
Three-strand wire with two-point wire barbs. Space between
pairs of barbs is greater than between barbs. Variation of
patent 157124.

642 Glidden's Barb, Three-strand Shell Variation
Three-strand wire with two-point, shell-like wire barb. Two
strands of equal gauge are reinforced with a smaller gauge
wire. Variation of patent 157124.

643 Glidden's Barb, Diminishing Strand Variation
Three-wire strands of different sizes with two-point wire barb.
Barb is mounted on the largest strand. Variation of patent
157124.

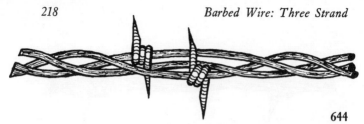

644
Glidden's Barb, Paired-barb Strands,
Three-strand Variation

Three-strand wire with two-point wire barbs. Paired barbs
are mounted separately on two of the three strands. Variation
of patent 157124.

Glidden's Barb, Parallel-wrap Variation   645

Three-strand wire with two-point wire barb. Barbed strand
is wrapped with parallel reinforcing strands. Variation of
patent 157124.

646
Glidden's Barb, Double Strand,
Reinforced Square-strand Variation

Three-strand wire with two-point wire barb. Barbed square
strand is reinforced with two twisted strands of round wire.
Variation of patent 157124.

647
Glidden's Barb, Double Strand, Reinforced
Round-strand Variation
Three-strand wire with two-point wire barb. Barbed strand is reinforced with twisted double strands. Variation of patent 157124.

648
Glidden's Barb, Double-barbed Strand,
Three-strand Variation
Three-strand wire with two-point wire barbs. Barbs are mounted separately on two strands. Variation of patent 157124.

Two-point Wire Barbs: *Wrap*

649
Brotherton's Barb, Three-strand Variation
Three-strand wire with two-point wire barb. Variation of patent 207710.

Two-point Wire Barbs: *Loop Locked*

650
Kelly's Swinging Barb,
Three Strand

Three-strand wire with two-point wire barb. Barb hangs from loop in the center strand. Patented [322108] July 14, 1885, by Michael Kelly of New York, N.Y.

Two-point Wire Barbs: *Strand Clutched*

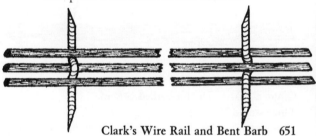

Clark's Wire Rail and Bent Barb   651

Three parallel single-wire strands with bent wire barbs. Material from molten metal bath holds barbs in place. Patented [254923] March 14, 1882, by Norman Clark of Sterling, Ill.

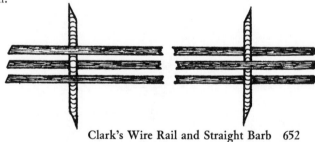

Clark's Wire Rail and Straight Barb   652

Three parallel single-wire strands with straight wire barbs. Material from molten metal bath holds barbs in place. Patented [254923] March 14, 1882, by Norman Clark of Sterling, Ill.

653 Upham's Three-loop Barb
Three-strand wire with two-point wire barb. Barb is bent and looped to receive strands. Patented [305356] September 16, 1884, by Andrew J. Upham of Sterling, Ill.

Two-point Wire Barbs: *Horizontal Strand Locking*

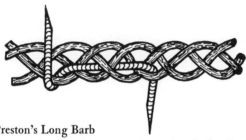

654 Preston's Long Barb
Three-strand braid with two-point wire barb. Patented [248348] October 18, 1881, by Othniel Preston of Hornellsville, N.Y.

Two-point Wire Barbs: *Integrated Barb Strand*

655 Mighell's Winding Barb, Three Strand
Three-strand wire with two strands continuous and the third cut to form barbs. Patented [199924] February 5, 1878, by Montraville P. Mighell of Delta, Iowa.

Nichols' Single Grip   656

Three-strand wire with one strand composed of wire sections
joined at ends to form barb. Patented [246191] August 23,
1881, by George W. Nichols of Coldwater, Mich.

Nichols' Reverse Grip   657

Three-strand wire with one strand composed of wire sections
joined at ends to form barb. Patented [246191] August 23,
1881, by George W. Nichols of Coldwater, Mich.

Nichols' Double Grip   658

Three-strand wire with one strand composed of wire sections
joined at ends to form barb. Patented [246191] August 23,
1881, by George W. Nichols of Coldwater, Mich.

659   Preston's Braid and Wrap Barb
Three-strand wire braid. One strand is composed of wire
sections joined at ends to form barbs. Patented [248348]
October 18, 1881, by Othniel Preston of Hornellsville, N.Y.

660   Washburn's Seated Barb, Three Strand
Three-strand wire with one strand composed of wire sections
joined at ends to form two-point barb. Patented [249212]
November 8, 1881, by Charles F. Washburn of Worcester,
Mass.

Four-point Wire Barbs: *Coil*

661
Edenborn's Double-straddle Barb,
Three-strand Variation
Three-strand wire with four-point
wire barb. Variation of patent 313929.

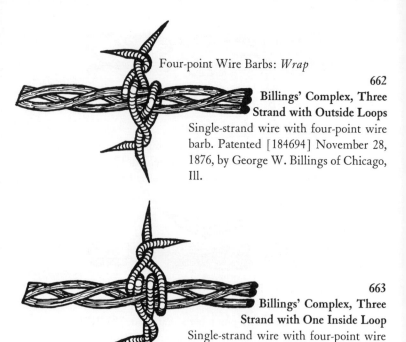

Four-point Wire Barbs: *Wrap*

662
**Billings' Complex, Three
Strand with Outside Loops**
Single-strand wire with four-point wire
barb. Patented [184694] November 28,
1876, by George W. Billings of Chicago,
Ill.

663
**Billings' Complex, Three
Strand with One Inside Loop**
Single-strand wire with four-point wire
barb. Patented [184694] November 28,
1876, by George W. Billings of Chicago,
Ill.

Cline's Rail   664
Three parallel single-wire strands with
four-point wire barb. Patented [290974]
December 25, 1883, by John B. Cline of
Jefferson, Iowa.

Four-point Wire Barbs: *Spreader*

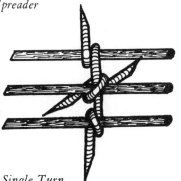

665 Ellwood's Three-strand Parallel and Tied Reverse
Three parallel single-wire strands with four-point wire barb. Patented [253022] January 31, 1882, by Abram Ellwood of Sycamore, Ill.

Two-point Sheet Metal Barbs: *Single Turn*

666 Baker's Barb, Three-strand Variation
Three-strand wire with two-point flat wire barb. Variation of patent 273219.

Two-point Sheet Metal Barbs: *Wrap*

667
Nadelhoffer's Flat-wire Gull Wing, Three Strand
Three-strand wire with flat two-point wire barb. Patented [307673] November 4, 1884, by John W. Nadelhoffer of Joliet, Ill.

Three-point Sheet Metal Barbs: *Vee Plate*

Wormley's Vee Plate   668

Three-strand wire with V-shaped, three-point sheet metal barb. Matching points of barb are wrapped in opposite directions around two strands. Patented [169393] November 2, 1875, by Abram V. Wormley of Cornton, Ill.

Wormley's Vee Plate, Spread-point Variation   669

Three-strand wire with three-point sheet metal barb. Variation of patent 169393.

Four-point Sheet Metal Barbs: *Joint Locked*

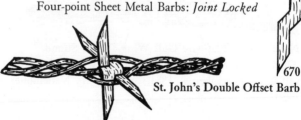

670

St. John's Double Offset Barb

Three-strand wire with four-point, two-piece sheet metal barb. Patented [205697] July 2, 1878, by Spencer H. and Justus M. St. John of Cedar Rapids, Iowa.

Four-point Sheet Metal Barbs: *Strand Clutched*

671   St. John's Double-vee Barb
Three-strand wire with four-point, two-piece sheet metal barb. Patented [205967] July 2, 1878, by Spencer H. and Justus M. St. John of Cedar Rapids, Iowa.

Four-point Sheet Metal Barbs: *Fence Strap*

672   Gore's Barb Strap
Two parallel three-strand cables with four-point sheet metal barb strap. Barb points are bent to lock in cable strands. Patented [294612] March 4, 1884, by Willis K. Gore of Johnstown, Pa.

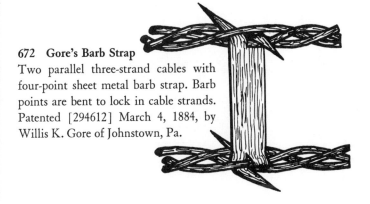

Multi-point Sheet Metal Barbs: *Star*

McGlin–Hart's Star   673

Three-strand wire with five-point sheet metal barb. Barb is perforated to receive strands. Patented [182212] September 12, 1876, by James C. McGlin and Thomas E. Hart of Shabbona Grove, Ill.

BARBED WIRE: Four Strand

Two-point Barbs: *Coil*

674

Glidden's Barb, Paired Barbs, Four-strand Variation
Four-strand wire with two-point wire barbs. Distance between pairs of barbs is greater than between barbs. Variation of patent 157124.

675

Glidden's Barb, Double-strand Wrap Variation
Four-strand wire with two-point wire barb. Barb is wrapped around two strands. Variation of patent 157124.

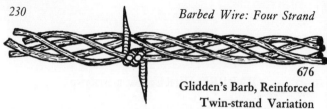

676

**Glidden's Barb, Reinforced
Twin-strand Variation**

Four-strand wire with two-point wire barb. The two small strands are equal in gauge, and the two larger strands unequal. Barb is mounted on a small strand. Variation of patent 157124.

Two-point Barbs: *Strand Clutched*

677

Ingraham's Barb and Visible Loop Wire Fencing

Four-strand visible wire fencing with two-point bent barb separated by loops in the strands. Patented [469062] February 16, 1892, by T. J. Ingraham of Hornellsville, N.Y.

Ingraham's Combined Barb and Visible Wire Fencing   678

Four-strand visible wire fencing with combination bent and loop barbs. Patented [469062] February 16, 1892, by T. J. Ingraham of Hornellsville, N.Y.

Two-point Barbs: *Double Tack*

679   Underwood's Double Tack
Three-strand wire with double-tack barb. Patented [206754]
August 6, 1878, by Henry M. Underwood of Kenosha, Wis.

Multi-point Sheet Metal Barbs: *Wheel*

680   Evans' Spur Wheel, Four Strand
Four-strand cable with eight-point sheet metal barb. Cable is
parted to cage barb and support pointed shaft and tie wire.
Patented [287261] October 23, 1883, by John Elias Evans of
Spanish Fork, Utah.

BARBED WIRE: LINK WIRE

Two-point Terminal Barbs: *End Tie and Loop*

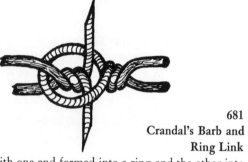

681
Crandal's Barb and
Ring Link

Wire link with one end formed into a ring and the other into a two-point barb. Barbs and rings join to form continuous fencing. Patented [184844] November 28, 1876, by Edward M. Crandal of Chicago, Ill.

682
Crandal's Link,
T-Loop Variation

Wire sections looped and joined at ends to form two-point barbs. Barbs and loops join to form continuous fencing. Variation of patent 184844.

232

683 Crandal's Link, End Twist Variation
Wire sections folded and twisted at ends to form link and two-point barbs. Barbs and loops are joined for continuous fencing. Variation of patent 184844.

Two-point Terminal Barbs: *Hook and Loop*

684 Hunt's Link
Wire sections folded, twisted, and shaped to form eyes and barbs. Barbs and eyes join to form continuous fencing. Patented [189861] April 24, 1877, by George G. Hunt of Bristol, Ill.

685 Crandal's Twist Link
Wire links joined and twisted to form two-point barbs and continuous fencing. Patented [240388] April 19, 1881, by Edward M. Crandal of Chicago, Ill.

Lewis' Link, Crossover Lock   686

Wire sections folded and joined at ends to form barbs and continuous fencing. Patented [465629] December 22, 1891, by Elliot E. Lewis of Troy, N.Y.

Lewis' Link, Simple Lock   687

Wire sections folded and joined at ends to form barbs and continuous fencing. Patented [465630] December 22, 1891, by Elliot E. Lewis of Troy, N.Y.

Griswold's Flyer   688

Wire sections folded and joined at ends to form barbs and continuous fencing. Patented [465638] December 22, 1891, by J. Wool Griswold of Troy, N.Y.

689 Griswold's Side Lock

Wire sections folded and joined at ends to form barbs and
continuous fencing. Patented [465639] December 22, 1891, by
J. Wool Griswold of Troy, N.Y.

690 Griswold's Folded Wing

Wire sections folded and joined to form barbs and continuous
fencing. Patented [465640] December 22, 1891, by J. Wool
Griswold of Troy, N.Y.

691 Griswold's Savage

Wire sections folded and joined at ends to form barbs and
continuous fencing. Barb points are perpendicular to flat side
of links. Patented [465641] December 22, 1891, by J. Wool
Griswold of Troy, N.Y.

Griswold's Sidewinder   692

Wire sections folded and joined at ends to form barbs and continuous fencing. Patented [465642] December 22, 1891, by
J. Wool Griswold of Troy, N.Y.

Griswold's Complex   693

Wire sections folded and joined at ends to form barbs and
continuous fencing. Patented [465643] December 22, 1891,
by J. Wool Griswold of Troy, N.Y.

Griswold's Inner Cross-tie   694

Wire sections folded and joined at ends to form barbs and
continuous fencing. Patented [465644] December 22, 1891, by
J. Wool Griswold of Troy, N.Y.

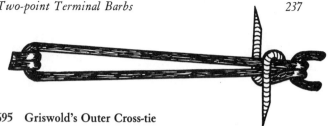

695 Griswold's Outer Cross-tie
Wire sections folded and joined at ends to form barbs and continuous fencing. Patented [465645] December 22, 1891, by J. Wool Griswold of Troy, N.Y.

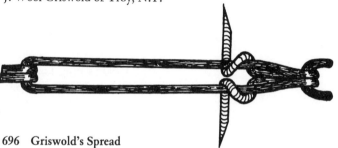

696 Griswold's Spread
Wire sections folded and joined at ends to form barb and continuous fencing. Patented [472496] April 5, 1892, by J. Wool Griswold of Troy, N.Y.

Two-point Terminal Barbs: *Coil and Loop*

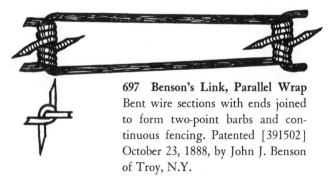

697 Benson's Link, Parallel Wrap
Bent wire sections with ends joined to form two-point barbs and continuous fencing. Patented [391502] October 23, 1888, by John J. Benson of Troy, N.Y.

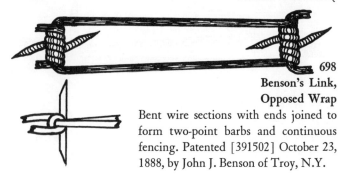

698
Benson's Link,
Opposed Wrap

Bent wire sections with ends joined to form two-point barbs and continuous fencing. Patented [391502] October 23, 1888, by John J. Benson of Troy, N.Y.

Two-point Terminal Barbs: *Center Wrap*

Parker's Ring Link   699

Wire section folded to center and fastened with wire ring. Ends of wire section form a two-point barb. Patented [194260] August 14, 1877, by Charles P. Parker of Joliet, Ill.

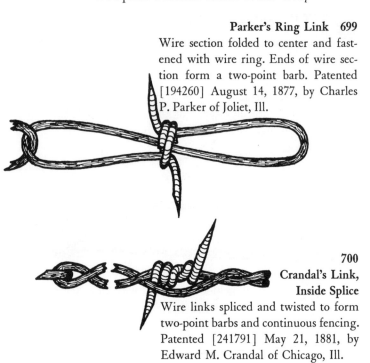

700
Crandal's Link,
Inside Splice

Wire links spliced and twisted to form two-point barbs and continuous fencing. Patented [241791] May 21, 1881, by Edward M. Crandal of Chicago, Ill.

701   Crandal's Link,
Outside-splice Variation
Barbed link looped and spliced at center to form two-point
barb. Loops join to form continuous fencing. Variation of
patent 241791.

702   Crandal's Link,
Simple Outside-splice Variation
Folded wire sections with ends joined in center to form barbs.
Loops join for continuous fencing. Variation of patent 241791.

703   Crandal's Link, Twist-loop Variation
Folded and twisted wire sections with ends joined in center
to form barbs. Loops join for continuous fencing. Variation
of patent 241791.

704
Crandal's Link, Compound Outside-splice Variation
Folded wire sections with ends joined in center to form barbs.
Loops join for continuous fencing. Variation of patent 241791.

705
Kay's Center Tie
Wire section folded and tied in center to form two-point barb.
Twisted links are joined at loops to form continuous fencing.
Patented [286987] October 16, 1883, by William V. Kay of
Waukegan, Ill.

706
McGill's Single-wire Link
Single-wire sections looped back and wrapped to form two-
point barb. Patented [343482] June 8, 1886, by George W.
McGill of New York, N.Y.

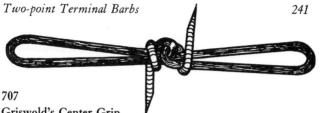

707
Griswold's Center Grip
Folded wire section with ends joined in the center to form
barb. Loops are joined to form continuous fencing. Patented
[486179] November 15, 1892, by J. Wool Griswold of Troy,
N.Y.

708
Griswold's Center Splice
Folded wire section with ends joined in the center to form
barb. Loops are joined to form continuous fencing. Patented
[486179] November 15, 1892, by J. Wool Griswold of Troy,
N.Y.

Two-point Terminal Barbs: *Diamond Plate*

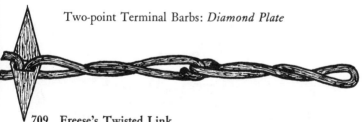

709   Freese's Twisted Link
Wire sections folded, joined in the center, and twisted. Ends
link in two-point sheet metal barb to form continuous fencing. Patented [383804] May 29, 1888, by Peter C. Freese of
Cayuga, N.Y.

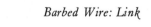

Freese's Straight Link   710

Wire sections folded and joined in center. Ends link in two-point sheet metal barb to form continuous fencing. Patented [383804] May 29, 1888, by Peter C. Freese of Cayuga, N.Y.

Four-point Terminal Barbs: *Center Wrap*

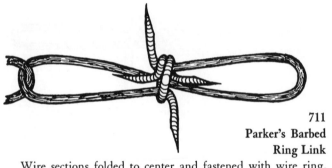

711
Parker's Barbed
Ring Link

Wire sections folded to center and fastened with wire ring. Ends of link and ring are bent to form a four-point barb. Patented [194260] August 14, 1877, by Charles P. Parker of Joliet, Ill.

712
McGill's Double-wire Link

Double-wire sections and four-point barb. Ends of sections

are looped back and wrapped to form barb. Patented [343482] June 8, 1886, by George W. McGill of New York, N.Y.

Four-point Terminal Barbs: *Hook and Diamond Plate*

713   Hunt's Plate-locked Link
Folded and twisted wire sections joined to form continuous fencing. Ends of wire section and diamond-shaped sheet metal locking plate form a four-point barb. Patented [193370] July 24, 1877, by George G. Hunt of Bristol, Ill.

Multi-point Terminal Barbs: *End Wrap*

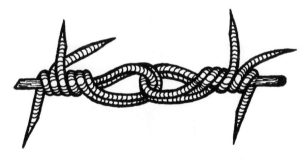

714   McGill's Link, Six-point Variation
Single-wire sections and six-point barb. Ends of sections with added wire pieces are looped back and wrapped to form barb. Variation of patent 343482.

Multi-point Terminal Barbs: *Wheel*

Whitney–Hubbell's Spur Wheel, Twisted Link   715

Bent and twisted wire sections joined to form continuous fencing. Twelve-point barb wheel moves on axle formed by bend in the link. Patented [344428] June 29, 1886, by Joel F. Whitney and Myron R. Hubbell of Wolcott, Vt.

Whitney–Hubbell's Spur Wheel, Straight Link   716

Bent wire sections joined to form continuous fencing. Twelve-point barb wheel moves on axle formed by bend in the link. Patented [344428] June 29, 1886, by Joel F. Whitney and Myron R. Hubbell of Wolcott, Vt.

717
Whitney–Hubbell's
Spur Wheel,
Center Tie

Folded wire sections with ends joined at center. Sections link to form continuous fencing. Twelve-point barb wheel moves on axle formed by cross wire in joint. Patented [344428] June 29, 1886, by Joel F. Whitney and Myron R. Hubbell of Wolcott, Vt.

BARBED WIRE: Sectional

Two-point Terminal Barbs: *Wrap*

718 Crandal's Folding Wire

Single-strand wire sections joined at ends to form two-point barbs and continuous fencing. Fencing is folded for transportation. Patented [174664] March 14, 1875, by Edward M. Crandal of Chicago, Ill.

719 Crandal's Folding Wire, Wrap Variation

Single-wire sections folded and joined at ends to form barbs and continuous fencing. Variation of patent 174664.

720 Brown's Link

Single-strand wire sections gripping at ends to form two-point barbs and continuous fencing. Patented [182351] September 19, 1876, by Rollin G. Brown of DeWitt, Iowa.

Evans' Twist Grip   721

Single-strand wire sections joined together at ends to form two-point barbs and continuous fencing. Patented [183552] October 24, 1876, by Lemuel E. Evans of New York, N.Y.

Hewitt's Twist   722

Single-strand wire looped and twisted to form barb body. Part of loop is cut away to form barb points. Patented [276039] April 17, 1883, by William Hewitt of Trenton, N.J.

Two-point Terminal Barbs: *Diamond Plate*

Hunt's Single-plate Locked Link   723

Single-wire sections hooked together at ends. One hook is locked with two-point, perforated sheet metal barb. The other is crimped or soldered. Patented [197729] December 4, 1877, by George G. Hunt of Bristol, Ill.

724
Cook's Link and Slotted Diamond

Wire sections with two-point sheet metal barbs. Ends of wire sections hook in barb slots to form continuous single-strand fencing. Patented [265025] September 26, 1882, by Joseph T. Cook of Chicago, Ill.

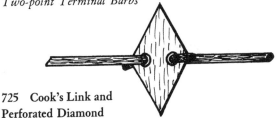

725   Cook's Link and Perforated Diamond

Wire sections with two-point sheet metal barbs. Ends of wire sections hook in holes in barbs to form continuous single-strand fencing. Patented [265025] September 26, 1882, by Joseph T. Cook of Chicago, Ill.

Two-point Terminal Barbs: *Hook*

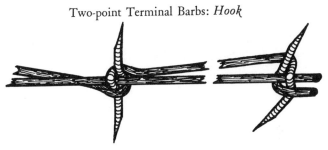

726   Hill's Riding Section

Single-strand wire with riding wire sections linked together at ends to form two-point barbs. Patented [182928] October 3, 1876, by Peter P. Hill of Alto, Ill.

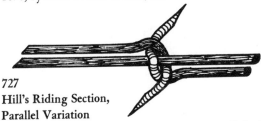

727
Hill's Riding Section, Parallel Variation

Single-strand wire with riding wire sections linked together at ends to form two-point barbs. Links are parallel to strand. Variation of patent 182928.

728
Sherman's Linked Rods
Wire sections joined at ends to form
two-point barbs and continuous fencing.
Barbs disconnect for storage or trans-
portation. Patented [221427] November
11, 1879, by Charles A. Sherman of
Boonesborough, Iowa.

Two-point Terminal Barbs: *Tie*

729
Bronson's Link,
One Strand
Single-wire sections joined to form two-
point barbs and continuous fencing.
Patented [189994] April 24, 1877, by
Adelbert E. Bronson of Chicago, Ill.

730
Steward's Square Knot
Single-strand wire sections with ends
joined in square knot to form two-point
barbs. Patented [191263] May 29, 1877,
by John F. Steward of Plano, Ill.

Tysdal's Hitch Tie   731
Single-strand wire sections joined at ends
with half hitches to form barbs. Patented
[208001] September 10, 1878, by Knud
Tysdal of Lee, Ill.

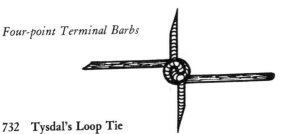

732 Tysdal's Loop Tie
Single-strand wire sections joined at ends with loops to form barbs. Patented [208001] September 10, 1878, by Knud Tysdal of Lee, Ill.

Two-point Terminal Barbs: *Triangle Plate*

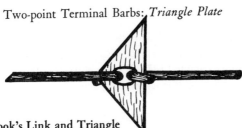

733 Cook's Link and Triangle
Wire sections with two-point sheet metal barbs. Ends of wire sections hook in barb slots to form continuous single-strand fencing. Patented [265025] September 26, 1882, by Joseph T. Cook of Chicago, Ill.

Four-point Terminal Barbs: *Diamond Plate*

734
Hunt's Double-plate
Locked Link
Single-wire sections hooked together at ends and locked with two perforated, diamond-shaped sheet metal barbs. Patented [197729] December 4, 1877, by George G. Hunt of Bristol, Ill.

Four-point Terminal Barbs: *Split Wire*

Sherman's Split Links   735

Wire sections joined at ends to form four-point barbs and continuous fencing. Links disconnect for storage or transportation. Patented [221427] November 11, 1879, by Charles A. Sherman of Boonesborough, Iowa.

Four-point Terminal Barbs: *Vee Plate*

Cook's Fin   736

Wire sections with two-point sheet metal barbs. Ends of wire sections hook in holes in barbs to form continuous single-strand fencing. Patented [265025] September 26, 1882, by Joseph T. Cook of Chicago, Ill.

BARBED WIRE: Mesh

Two-point Wire Barbs: *Single Turn*

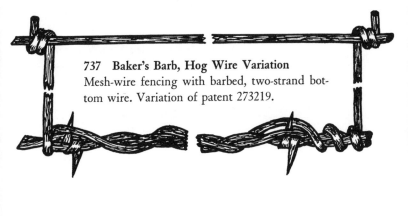

737   Baker's Barb, Hog Wire Variation
Mesh-wire fencing with barbed, two-strand bottom wire. Variation of patent 273219.

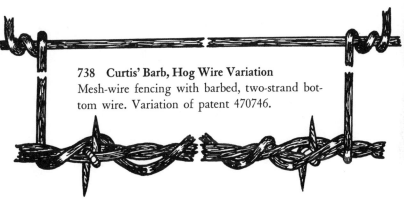

738   Curtis' Barb, Hog Wire Variation
Mesh-wire fencing with barbed, two-strand bottom wire. Variation of patent 470746.

Two-point Wire Barbs: *Coil*

Glidden's Barb, Hog Wire Variation   739

Mesh hog wire with barbed-wire reinforcement at the base.
Variation of patent 157124.

Two-point Wire Barbs: *Loop Locked*

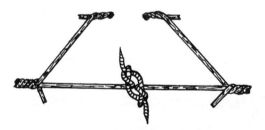

Evans' Barbed Mesh   740

Hexagonal wire mesh with interlocking wire barb. Patented
[255728] March 28, 1882, by Lemuel E. Evans of East Orange,
N.J.

Two-point Wire Barbs: *Spreader*

741 Decker's Barbed Mesh
Horizontal wire strands with barbed vertical wire sections.
Patented [186716] January 30, 1877, by Alexander C. Decker
of Bushnell, Ill.

742 Decker's Barbed Mesh with Double-strand Bottom Wire
Horizontal wire strands with barbed vertical wire sections.
Patented [186716] January 30, 1877, by Alexander C. Decker
of Bushnell, Ill.

Four-point Wire Barbs: *Coil*

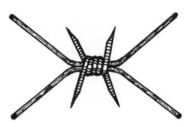

Glidden's Coils, Mesh-wire Variation   743
Mesh wire with four-point wire barbs. Barbs mounted at
intersections join the wire panels. Variation of reissue patent
6914.

Four-point Wire Barbs: *Swinging*

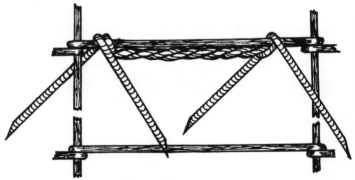

Pearson's Four-point Swinging Barb   744
Mesh wire with four-point wire barbs strung horizontally
along the middle strand. Patented [403774] May 21, 1889, by
Alfred N. Pearson of Northcote, British Colony of Victoria.

Multi-point Wire Barbs: *Swinging*

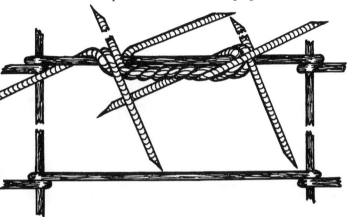

745   Pearson's Multi-point Swinging Barb
Mesh wire with eight-point wire barbs strung horizontally
along the middle strand. Patented [403774] May 21, 1889, by
Alfred N. Pearson of Northcote, British Colony of Victoria.

Four-point Sheet Metal Barbs: *Star*

746   Weaver's Barbed-mesh Fencing
Mesh wire with four-point star barb. Barb is placed in fencing
with face either horizontal, vertical, or in combination.
Patented [220740] October 21, 1879, by James H. Weaver of
Chicago, Ill.

BARBED WIRE: Interlaced Fence Strands

Two-point Wire Barbs: *Hook*

Bestor's Wrapped Strands   747

Four-wire fencing of single strands with wire wraps and
loops. Loops are joined with two-point wire barbs. Patented
[197757] December 4, 1877, by Francis L. Bestor of Oskaloosa, Iowa.

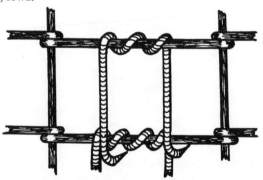

Pearson's Two-point Swinging Barb   748

Mesh wire with two-point wire barbs. Wire is designed for

either barrier or trap fencing. Patented [403774] May 21, 1889, by Alfred N. Pearson of Northcote, British Colony of Victoria.

Two-point Wire Barbs: *Spreader*

749   Bestor's Tied Strands
Four-wire fencing of single strands with interlocking wire loops. Ends of loops wrap around strands and form barbs. Patented [197757] December 4, 1877, by Francis L. Bestor of Oskaloosa, Iowa.

Section II. Metallic Strip Fencing

Metallic strip fencing was as well suited to the prairies and plains of the western states as was wire fencing. Like that of wire fencing, its supply was unlimited; however, it could be produced from sheet metal more cheaply than fencing made from wire. Its designs were as simple and effective as barbed wire in pricking the skin of men, tearing the flesh of cattle and horses, or pulling the wool of sheep. It was also easy to install and easy to move, and it could be repaired or rebuilt readily when damaged.

Barbs and strips could be stamped or cut in one piece, or the barbs could be mounted separately. Although one strip appeared adequate, occasionally a wire or another strip was added to give it greater strength. Usually made of light gauge sheet metal, strip fencing was flexible, strong, and capable of maintaining its tautness during hot or cold weather. The inventors of metallic strip fencing maintained that it was ornamental and more visible to livestock.

Well-known inventors who exploited this type of fencing were Thomas V. Allis, Jacob and Warren M. Brinkerhoff, William E. Brock, and Franklin D. Ford.

BARBLESS STRIPS

Flat Strips: *Plain*

750 Metallic Fencing Strip
Sheet metal fencing. Metal strip remains in a flat position when installed in a fence.

751 Metallic Fencing Strip
Sheet metal fencing. Metal strip remains in a flat position when installed in a fence.

Flat Strips: *Ribbed*

752 Ribbed Metallic Fencing Strip
Sheet metal fencing. Reinforcing ribs run down edges and center on one side of strip. Other side is flat.

Woodard's Teardrop-edge Fencing Strip   753
Sheet metal strip with teardrop beading along edges. Patented
[462887] November 10, 1891, by Alonzo B. Woodard of
Hornellsville, N.Y.

Flat Strips: *Panel*

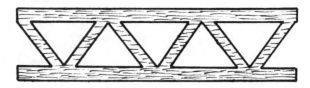

Kilmer's Window Strip   754
Ornamental sheet metal strip with triangular openings.
Patented [317799] May 12, 1885, by Irving A. and Melvin D.
Kilmer of Schenectady, N.Y.

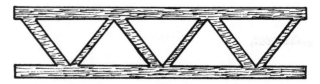

Kilmer's Window Strip, Small-leg Variation   755
Ornamental sheet metal strip with triangular openings. Variation of patent 317799.

756 Kilmer's Window Strip, Four-side Variation
Ornamental sheet metal strip with four-sided openings. Variation of patent 317799.

757 Kilmer's Window Strip, Bell-wire Variation
Ornamental sheet metal strip with bell-shaped openings. Variation of patent 317799.

Flat Strips: *Wire Reinforced*

758 Mann's Barbless Wire Strip Fencing
Combination grooved sheet metal strip and wire. Strip and wire are joined with sheet metal clips. Patented [266705] October 31, 1882, by Charles A. Mann of Buffalo, N.Y.

Flat Strips: *Undulating*

Gregg's Snake Wire   759

Single-strand undulating oval wire. Patented [441005] November 18, 1890, by Samuel H. Gregg of Crawfordsville, Ind.

Twist Strips: *Plain*

Twisted Metallic Fencing Strip   760

Twisted sheet metal fencing. Twist provides for expansion and contraction.

Flat-twist Metallic Fencing Strip   761

Sheet metal fencing. Strip has alternating flat and twisted sections.

Twisted Metallic Fencing Strip   762

Twisted sheet metal fencing. Twist provides for expansion and contraction.

Twist Strips: *Center Core*

763 Center-core Metallic Fencing Strip
Twisted sheet metal fencing. Strip has center core for reinforcement. Twist provides for expansion and contraction.

764 Square-ribbed Metallic Strip
Sheet metal fencing strip with a square reinforcing rib through the center.

Corrugated Strips: *Plain*

765 Fluted Ribbon Wire
Corrugated sheet metal fencing strip. Strip is reinforced with three longitudinal flutes.

766 Massey's Swaged Rail
Twisted oval-shaped metal strip with swaged sharpened edges. Patented [261619] July 25, 1882, by Ward E. Massey of Dubuque, Iowa.

Woodard's Diagonally-corrugated Fencing Strip   767

Corrugated sheet metal fencing strip. Patented [462887] November 10, 1891, by Alonzo B. Woodard of Hornellsville, N.Y.

Woodard's Ripple-corrugated Fencing Strip   768

Corrugated sheet metal fencing strip. Patented [462887] November 10, 1891, by Alonzo B. Woodard of Hornellsville, N.Y.

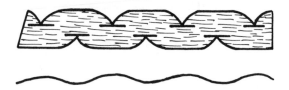

Allis' Ripple Strip   769

Corrugated sheet metal strip with circular-cut edges. Slit across notch reduces break tendency. Patented [486173] November 15, 1892, by Thomas V. Allis of New York, N.Y.

Corrugated Strips: *Ribbed*

770   Woodard's Diagonally-corrugated, Bead-edge Fencing Strip
Corrugated sheet metal strip with beaded edges. Patented [462887] November 10, 1891, by Alonzo B. Woodard of Hornellsville, N.Y.

771   Woodard's Diagonally-corrugated, Teardrop-edge Fencing Strip
Corrugated sheet metal strips with teardrop beading along edges. Patented [462887] November 10, 1891, by Alonzo B. Woodard of Hornellsville, N.Y.

772   Perkins' Crimp-edge Metallic Strip
Sheet metal strip with crimped and folded edges. Strip is perforated down the center. Patented [478170] July 5, 1892, by Richard B. Perkins of Hornellsville, N.Y.

Sectional Strips: *Plate Locked*

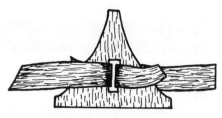

773

Milligan's Scrap Metal Fencing, Front and Back Clinch
Metal straps hooked through opening in three-point metal
plate to form continuous cable. Patented [268264] November
28, 1882, by John C. Milligan of Brooklyn, N.Y.

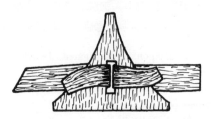

774

Milligan's Scrap Metal Fencing, Front Clinch
Metal straps hooked through opening in three-point metal
plate to form continuous cable. Patented [268264] November
28, 1882, by John C. Milligan of Brooklyn, N.Y.

775

Milligan's Scrap Metal Fencing, Double Tension-locked
Metal straps hooked through opening in three-point metal

plate to form continuous cable. Ends of plate fold to keep cable from parting. Patented [268264] November 28, 1882, by John C. Milligan of Brooklyn, N.Y.

776   Milligan's Scrap Metal Fencing, Tension-locked
Metal straps hooked through opening in three-point metal plate to form continuous cable. Large end of plate is folded to keep cable from parting. Patented [268264] November 28, 1882, by John C. Milligan of Brooklyn, N.Y.

777   Brock's Sectional Metallic Strip
Sheet metal strips joined to form continuous fencing. Ends of strip are notched and washer-locked. Patented [344077] June 22, 1886, by Adeline Brock of Dunnellen, N.J.

BARB-MOUNTED STRIPS

One-point Barbs: *Tack*

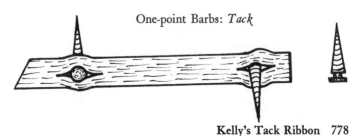

Kelly's Tack Ribbon   778

Sheet metal strip and tack barbs. Strip is slit at intervals to receive tacks. Patented [84062] November 17, 1868, by Michael Kelly of New York, N.Y.

Baker's Tack Rail   779

Folded sheet metal strip with tack barbs. Pressure along folded edges holds tacks in the channel. Patented [256535] April 18, 1882, by George C. Baker of Des Moines, Iowa.

Upham's Tack Strip   780

Sheet metal strip with tack barbs. Serrated edge of strip is folded over to hold tacks. Patented [272923] February 27, 1883, by Andrew J. Upham of Sycamore, Ill.

One-point Barbs: *Sprig*

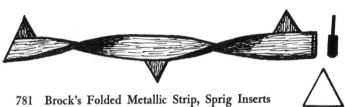

781 Brock's Folded Metallic Strip, Sprig Inserts
Folded and twisted sheet metal strip with triangular sheet
metal barb inserts. Patented [305282] September 16, 1884, by
William E. Brock of New York, N.Y.

Two-point Barbs: *Single Turn*

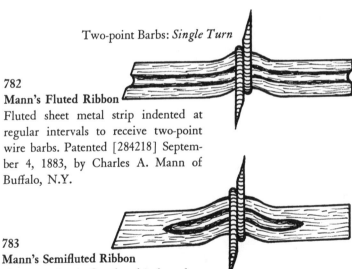

782
Mann's Fluted Ribbon
Fluted sheet metal strip indented at
regular intervals to receive two-point
wire barbs. Patented [284218] September 4, 1883, by Charles A. Mann of
Buffalo, N.Y.

783
Mann's Semifluted Ribbon
Sheet metal strip fluted and indented at
regular intervals to receive two-point
wire barbs. Patented [284218] September 4, 1883, by Charles A. Mann of
Buffalo, N.Y.

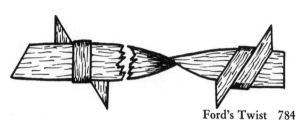

Ford's Twist   784

Twisted sheet metal strip with two-point sheet metal barb. Barb is wrapped around and crimped to strip. Patented [319807] June 9, 1885, by Franklin D. Ford of Providence, R.I.

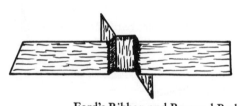

Ford's Ribbon and Recessed Barb   785

Sheet metal strip with two-point sheet metal barb. Strip is depressed at intervals to hold barb in place. Patented [319807] June 9, 1885, by Franklin D. Ford of Providence, R.I.

Ford's Twist and Staggered Offset Barb   786

Twisted sheet metal strip with two-point sheet metal barb. Barb is wrapped around and crimped to strip. Patented [319807] June 9, 1885, by Franklin D. Ford of Providence, R.I.

787   Ford's Twist and Offset Barb
Twisted sheet metal strip with two-point sheet metal barb.
Barb is wrapped around and crimped to strip. Patented
[319807] June 9, 1885, by Franklin D. Ford of Providence, R.I.

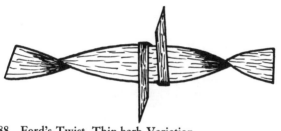

788   Ford's Twist, Thin-barb Variation
Twisted sheet metal strip with two-point sheet metal barb.
Narrow barb strip is wrapped around and crimped to strip.
Variation of patent 319807.

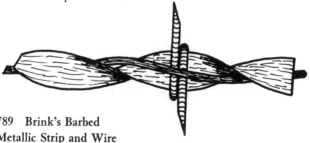

**789   Brink's Barbed
Metallic Strip and Wire**
Wire and metallic strip fencing with two-point wire barb.
Barb is mounted on the metallic strip. Patented [324221]
August 11, 1885, by John J. Brinkerhoff of Auburn, N.Y.

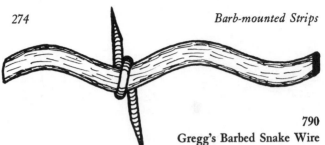

790
Gregg's Barbed Snake Wire

Single-strand undulating wire with two-point wire barb. Patented [441005] November 18, 1890, by Samuel H. Gregg of Crawfordsville, Ind.

Two-point Barbs: *Coil*

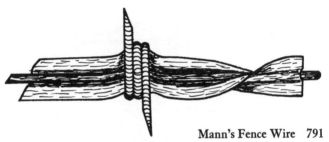

Mann's Fence Wire   791

Combination grooved sheet metal strip. Fencing is bent at intervals to receive suitable type barb. Patented [266705] October 31, 1882, by Charles A. Mann of Buffalo, N.Y.

792
Brink's Barbed Wire and Metallic Strip

Wire and metallic strip fencing with two-point wire barb. Barb is mounted on the wire. Patented [324221] August 11, 1885, by John J. Brinkerhoff of Auburn, N.Y.

**793   Brink's Barbed Wire
and Metallic Strip, Double-strand Variation**
Two-strand wire and metallic strip with two-point wire barb.
Variation of patent 324221.

Two-point Barbs: *Twist*

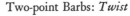

794   Nellis' Twist
Sheet metal strip with two-point wire barb. Two pieces of
wire are bent around strip and twisted to form barb. Patented
[191993] June 12, 1877, by Aaron J. Nellis of Pittsburgh, Pa.

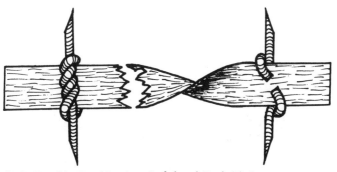

795   Brink's Combination, Left-hand Barb Twist
Twisted sheet metal strip with two-point, twisted wire barb.
Patented [219143] September 2, 1879, by Jacob and Warren
M. Brinkerhoff of Auburn, N.Y.

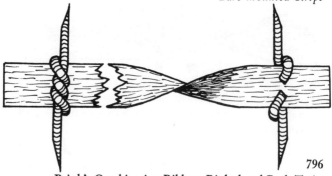

796

Brink's Combination Ribbon, Right-hand Barb Twist
Twisted sheet metal strip with two-point, twisted wire barb.
Patented [219143] September 2, 1879, by Jacob and Warren
M. Brinkerhoff of Auburn, N.Y.

Potts' Metallic Fencing   797
Sheet metal strip with two-point wire barbs. Strip is notched
to receive barbs. Patented [296060] April 1, 1884, by Albert
Potts of Philadelphia, Pa.

Trevitt–Mouck's Turnstile Two Point   798
Sheet metal strip with two-point wire barb. Barb rotates in
cage formed from slits cut in the strip. Patented [404879]
June 11, 1889, by Constant S. Trevitt and Solomon F. Mouck
of Lincoln, Nebr.

Two-point Barbs: *Clip*

**799 Nellis' Rail
with Spring-clip Barb**
Metallic strip with spring-clip barbs mounted at intervals
along one edge. Patented [191011] May 22, 1877, by Aaron J.
Nellis of Pittsburgh, Pa.

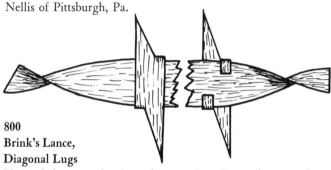

**800

Brink's Lance,
Diagonal Lugs**
Twisted sheet metal strip with two-point, clip-on sheet metal
barb. Patented [214095] April 8, 1879, by Jacob Brinkerhoff
of Auburn, N.Y.

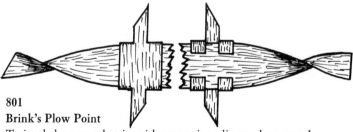

**801
Brink's Plow Point**
Twisted sheet metal strip with two-point, clip-on sheet metal
barb. Patented [214095] April 8, 1879, by Jacob Brinkerhoff
of Auburn, N.Y.

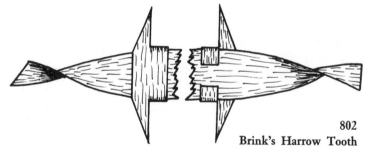

802
Brink's Harrow Tooth

Twisted sheet metal strip with two-point, clip-on sheet metal barb. Patented [214095] April 8, 1879, by Jacob Brinkerhoff of Auburn, N.Y.

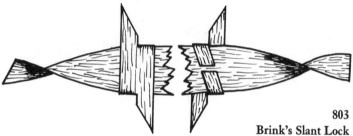

803
Brink's Slant Lock

Twisted sheet metal strip with two-point, clip-on sheet metal barb. Patented [214095] April 8, 1879, by Jacob Brinkerhoff of Auburn, N.Y.

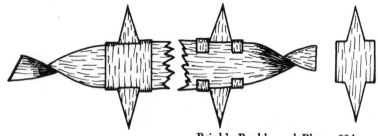

Brink's Buckle and Plate   804

Twisted sheet metal strip with two-piece, two-point, clip-on sheet metal barb. Clamp with four lugs holds shouldered

plate to strip. Patented [214095] April 8, 1879, by Jacob
Brinkerhoff of Auburn, N.Y.

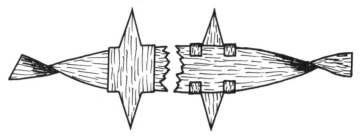

805 Brink's Buckle, One-piece Variation
Twisted sheet metal strip with two-point, clip-on sheet metal
barb. Variation of patent 214095.

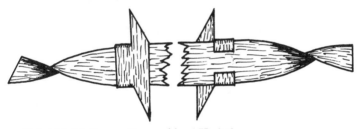

806 Brink's Lance, Opposed-lugs Variation
Twisted sheet metal strip with two-point, clip-on sheet metal
barb. Variation of patent 214095.

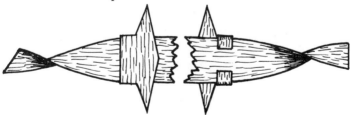

807 Brink's Buckle, Two-lug Variation
Twisted sheet metal strip with two-point, clip-on sheet metal
barb. Variation of patent 214095.

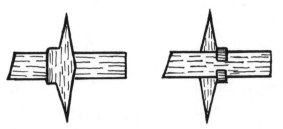

Brink's Buckle, Two-lug, Flat-strip Variation 808
Flat sheet metal strip with two-point, clip-on sheet metal barb.
Variation of patent 214095.

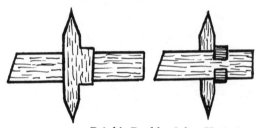

Brink's Buckle, Saber Variation 809
Flat sheet metal strip with two-point, clip-on sheet metal
barb. Variation of patent 214095.

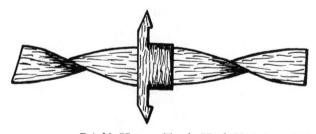

Brink's Harrow Tooth, Hook Variation 810
Twisted sheet metal strip with two-point, clamp-on sheet
metal barb. Variation of patent 214095.

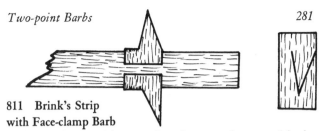

**811   Brink's Strip
with Face-clamp Barb**

Sheet metal strip with two-point, clamp-on sheet metal barb.
Patented [241601] May 17, 1881, by Jacob and Warren M.
Brinkerhoff of Auburn, N.Y.

**812
Elsey's Ribbon**

Sheet metal strip with two-point wire barb. Sheet metal plate
clipped to strip holds barb in place. Patented [265223] September 26, 1882, by George Elsey of Springfield, Mass.

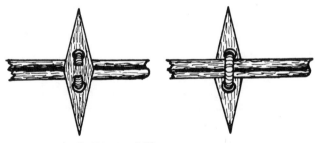

813   Devendorf's Diamond Plate

S-shaped sheet metal strip with two-point sheet metal barb.
Perforated barb is held in position with wire clip. Patented
[272534] February 20, 1883, by Henry A. Devendorf of Port
Jackson, N.Y.

Scutt's Ribbed Rail   814

Ribbed sheet metal strip with two-point metal barb. Barb is
pressed on metal strip. Patented [287059] October 23, 1883,
by Hiram B. Scutt of Joliet, Ill.

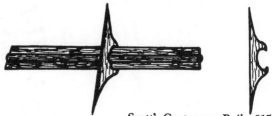

Scutt's Center-core Rail   815

Center-core, reinforced sheet metal strip with two-point metal
barb. Barb is pressed on metal strip. Variation of patent
287059.

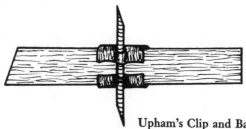

Upham's Clip and Barb   816

Sheet metal strip with two-point wire barb and clip. Per-
forated clip is crimped around barb and strip when mounted.
Patented [301187] July 1, 1884, by Andrew J. Upham of
Sycamore, Ill.

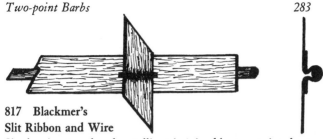

**817 Blackmer's
Slit Ribbon and Wire**
Single-wire strand and metallic strip joined by two-point sheet
metal barb. Barb passes around the wire and through slot in
strip. Spread points hold the barb in place. Patented [305277]
September 16, 1884, by Francis A. Blackmer of Springfield,
Mass.

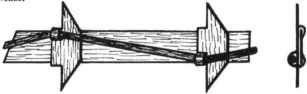

818 Blackmer's Strip and Front Reinforcing Wire
Sheet metal strip with two-point, clip-on sheet metal barb.
One lug on each barb grips both reinforcing wire and edge of
strip. Patented [307005] October 21, 1884, by Francis A.
Blackmer of Springfield, Mass.

819 Blackmer's Strip and Back Reinforcing Wire
Sheet metal strip with two-point, clip-on sheet metal barb.
One lug on each barb grips both reinforcing wire and edge
of strip. Patented [307005] October 21, 1884, by Francis A.
Blackmer of Springfield, Mass.

Two-point Barbs: *Insert*

Kelly's Ribbon and Wire Insert   820

Sheet metal strip with two-point wire barb. Strip is slit at regular intervals to receive barbs. Patented [84062] November 17, 1868, by Michael Kelly of New York, N.Y.

Kelly's Ribbon and Pin Insert   821

Sheet metal strip with two-point pin barbs. Strip is slit at intervals to receive barbs. Patented [84062] November 17, 1868, by Michael Kelly of New York, N.Y.

822

Kelly's Ribbon, Sheet Metal Barb Insert Variation

Sheet metal strip with two-point sheet metal barbs. Strip is slit to receive barbs. Variation of patent 84062.

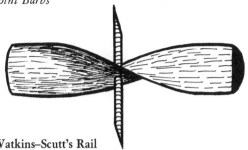

823 Watkins–Scutt's Rail
Half-round metal strip with two-point wire barb. Barb is inserted through hole in strip. Patented [163955] June 1, 1875, by William Watkins and Hiram B. Scutt of Joliet, Ill.

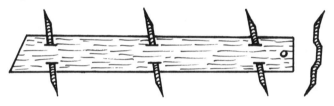

824 Gilman's Fence Bar
Sheet metal strip with two-point wire barbs. Strip is slit to receive barb inserts. Patented [182817] October 3, 1876, by William H. Gilman of Belvidere, Ill.

825 Judson's Metallic Strip
Perforated sheet metal strip with two-point wire barb inserts. Patented [191348] May 29, 1877, by Lyman P. Judson of E. New Market, Md.

Betts' Ribbon and Diamond   826

Slotted sheet metal strip with sheet metal insert barbs. Twist
in barb on each side of strip holds it in place. Patented
[199018] January 8, 1878, by Lewis F. Betts of Chicago, Ill.

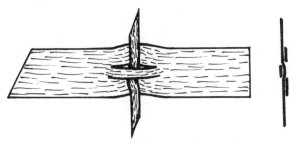

Upham's Ribbon and Insert   827

Sheet metal strip with narrow sheet metal barb. Slits are cut in
strip to receive barbs. Patented [255399] March 21, 1882, by
Andrew J. Upham of Sterling, Ill.

Harris' Ribbon   828

Sheet metal strip with two-point wire barb. Barb loops
through slot cut in the metal strip. Patented [258914] June 6,
1882, by William M. Harris of Menlo, Iowa.

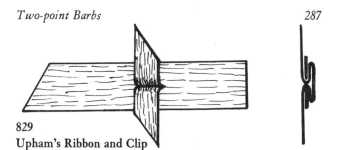

829
Upham's Ribbon and Clip
Sheet metal strip with two-point sheet metal barb. Folded barb is inserted through slit in strip and pressed in position. Patented [280100] June 28, 1883, by Andrew J. Upham of Sterling, Ill.

830
Upham's Ribbon and Fastener, Wire Reinforced
Sheet metal strip with two-point sheet metal barb. Strip is slit to receive barbs. Barbs hold strip and wire together. Variation of patent 280100.

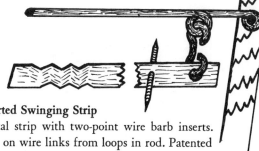

831
Kelly's Rod-supported Swinging Strip
Rippled sheet metal strip with two-point wire barb inserts. Strip swings freely on wire links from loops in rod. Patented [283614] August 21, 1883, by Michael Kelly of New York, N.Y.

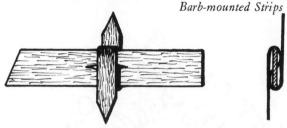

Upham's Slit Ribbon and Barb Insert   832

Sheet metal strip with two-point sheet metal barb. Barb passes
through slot and around edges of the strip. Patented [305354]
September 16, 1884, by Andrew J. Upham of Sterling, Ill.

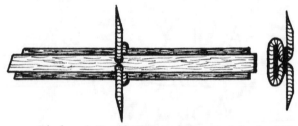

Blackmer's Double Strip and Wire Barb Lock   833

Sheet metal main strip and perforated reinforcing strip with
two-point wire barb. Barb. passes around main strip and
through holes in the reinforcing strip. Patented [307005]
October 21, 1884, by Francis A. Blackmer of Springfield, Mass.

Burtis' Ribbon   834

Sheet metal strip with sheet metal barb inserts. Strip is slit at
regular intervals to receive barbs. Patented [309924] December 30, 1884, by William Burtis of New Egypt, N.J.

Two-point Barbs: *Crimp Locked*

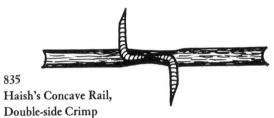

835
Haish's Concave Rail,
Double-side Crimp
Concave sheet metal strip with wire barb. Sides of strip are crimped against body of barb. Patented [332393] December 15, 1885, by Jacob Haish of De Kalb, Ill.

836   Haish's Concave Rail, Parallel Barb Points
Concave sheet metal strip with wire barb. One side of strip crimps over the body of the barb. Patented [332393] December 15, 1885, by Jacob Haish of De Kalb, Ill.

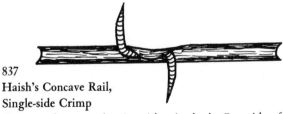

837
Haish's Concave Rail,
Single-side Crimp
Concave sheet metal strip with wire barb. One side of strip crimps over the body of the barb. Patented [332393] December 15, 1885, by Jacob Haish of De Kalb, Ill.

Four-point Barbs: *Twist*

Trevitt–Mouck's Turnstile Twist   838

Sheet metal strip with four-point wire barb. Barb rotates in cage formed from slits cut in the strip. Patented [404879] June 11, 1889, by Constant S. Trevitt and Solomon F. Mouck of Lincoln, Nebr.

Trevitt–Mouck's Turnstile Wrap   839

Sheet metal strip with four-point wire barb. Barb rotates in cage formed from slits cut in the strip. Patented [404879] June 11, 1889, by Constant S. Trevitt and Solomon F. Mouck of Lincoln, Nebr.

Four-point Barbs: *Clip*

840 Mouck's Three-to-one Barb, Metallic Strip
Sheet metal strip with four-point wire barb. Barb is held in place with clip-on sheet metal plate. Patented [507088] October 17, 1893, by Solomon F. Mouck of Denver, Colo.

Four-point Barbs: *Rider*

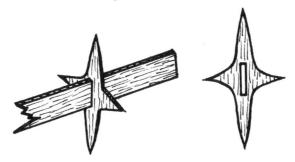

841 Ford's Elongated Star
Sheet metal strip with four-point, perforated sheet metal barb. Barb is crimped to strip. Patented [181328] August 22, 1876, by Robert Ford of Providence, R.I.

Four-point Barbs: *Insert*

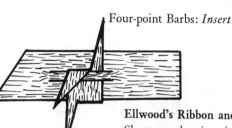

842

Ellwood's Ribbon and Offset Vee Barb
Sheet metal strip with four-point sheet
metal barb. Slit is cut in strip to receive
and hold barb in place. Patented
[147756] February 24, 1874, by Isaac L.
Ellwood of De Kalb, Ill.

843

Ellwood's Ribbon and Center-vee Barb
Sheet metal strip with four-point sheet
metal barb. Slit is cut in strip to receive
and hold barb in place. Patented
[147756] February 24, 1874, by Isaac L.
Ellwood of De Kalb, Ill.

844

Ellwood's Ribbon and Side-vee Barb
Sheet metal strip with four-point sheet
metal barb. Slit is cut in strip to receive
and hold barb in place. Patented
[147756] February 24, 1874, by Isaac L.
Ellwood of De Kalb, Ill.

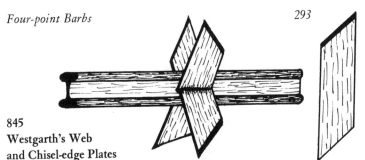

845
**Westgarth's Web
and Chisel-edge Plates**
Webbed strands with four-point sheet metal barb. Barb parts
are pushed through slot in web and spread at right angles.
Patented [239128] March 22, 1881, by John Westgarth of
Warrington, Eng.

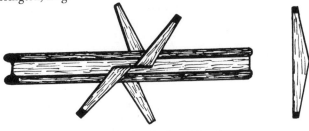

846 Westgarth's Web and Chisel-edge Triangle
Webbed strands with four-point sheet metal barb. Barb parts
are pushed through slot in web and spread at right angles.
Patented [239128] March 22, 1881, by John Westgarth of
Warrington, Eng.

**847 Westgarth's Web and
Chisel-edge Barb Strip**
Webbed strands with two-point sheet
metal barb. Barb parts are pushed
through slot in web and spread at right
angles. Patented [239128] March 22,
1881, by John Westgarth of Warrington, Eng.

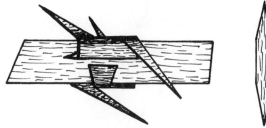 

Roberts' Ribbon and Double-clip Insert   848
Sheet metal strip with four-point sheet metal barb. Barb is inserted through slit in ribbon and fastened by lugs. Patented [276883] May 1, 1883, by William S. Roberts of Bolivar, N.Y.

Four-point Barbs: *Crimp Locked*

Haish's Concave Rail and Split Barb Plate   849
Concave sheet metal strip with four-point sheet metal barb. Sides of strip are crimped to the body of the barb. Patented [332393] December 15, 1885, by Jacob Haish of De Kalb, Ill.

Four-point Barbs: *Riveted*

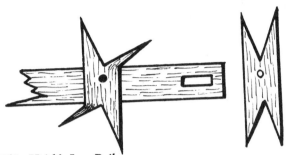

850   Haish's Iron Rail
Sheet metal strip with four-prong sheet metal barb plate. Barb
plate is riveted to strip. Patented [147634] February 17, 1874,
by Jacob Haish of De Kalb, Ill.

Multi-point Barbs: *Serrated Insert Strip*

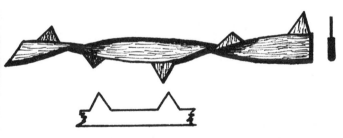

851   Brock's Folded Metallic Strip, Spaced Barb Plate
Folded and twisted sheet metal strip with spaced barb-plate
insert. Patented [305283] September 16, 1884, by William E.
Brock of New York, N.Y.

Brock's Folded Metallic Strip, Saw-tooth Insert   852
Folded and twisted sheet metal strip with saw-tooth insert.
Patented [305283] September 16, 1884, by William E. Brock
of New York, N.Y.

Multi-point Barbs: *Wheel*

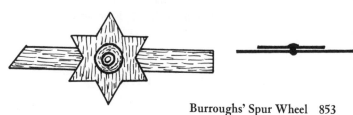

Burroughs' Spur Wheel   853
Sheet metal strip with six-point sheet metal barb. Barb is free
to rotate. Face of strip and barb lie in a horizontal position in
fencing. Patented [219067] September 2, 1879, by Henry R.
Burroughs of Chicago, Ill.

Fisher's Spur Wheel and Wire Shaft   854
Twisted sheet metal strip with slots cut at intervals to receive

sixteen-point sheet metal barb wheels. Barb wheel rotates on
wire shaft bent around edges of strip. Patented [373772]
November 22, 1887, by George P. Fisher, Jr. of Chicago, Ill.

855   Fisher's Spur Wheel

Twisted sheet metal strip with slots cut at intervals to receive
sixteen-point sheet metal barb wheels. Barb wheel rotates on
shaft projecting from strip. Shaft is clipped at one end for
mounting wheel. Patented [373772] November 22, 1887, by
George P. Fisher, Jr. of Chicago, Ill.

BARB-MOUNTED DOUBLE STRIPS

Two-point Barbs: *Clip*

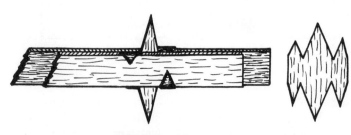

Childs' Double Strip with Four-lug Plate   856
Doubled sheet metal strips with two-point sheet metal barb. Lugs on barb hold strips together. Barb is mounted between the strips. Patented [285229] September 18, 1883, by J. Wallace Childs of Chicago, Ill.

Childs' Twisted Double Strip with Four-lug Plate   857
Doubled sheet metal strips with two-point sheet metal barb. Lugs on barbs hold strips together. Barb is mounted between the strips. Patented [285229] September 18, 1883, by J. Wallace Childs of Chicago, Ill.

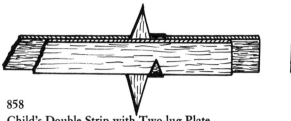

858
Child's Double Strip with Two-lug Plate
Doubled sheet metal strips with two-point sheet metal barb.
Lugs on barb hold strips together. Barb is mounted between
the strips. Patented [285229] September 18, 1883, by J. Wal-
lace Childs of Chicago, Ill.

859
Childs' Twisted Double Strip with Two-lug Plate
Doubled sheet metal strips with two-point sheet metal barb.
Lugs on barbs hold strips together. Barb is mounted between
the strips. Patented [285229] September 18, 1883, by J. Wal-
lace Childs of Chicago, Ill.

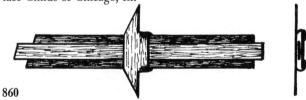

860
Blackmer's Double Strip and Clip-on Barb
Sheet metal main strip and reinforcing strip with two-point
sheet metal barb. Barb clips around both strips. Patented
[307005] October 21, 1884, by Francis A. Blackmer of Springfield, Mass.

Two-point Barbs: *Insert*

861

Blackmer's Double Strip and Two-lug Barb Lock
Sheet metal main strip and slit reinforcing strip with two-
point sheet metal barb. Barb is mounted between the two
strips. Lugs on barb pass through slits in reinforcing strip, and
clip to the main strip. Patented [307005] October 21, 1884, by
Francis A. Blackmer of Springfield, Mass.

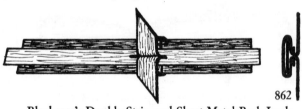

862

Blackmer's Double Strip and Sheet Metal Barb Lock
Sheet metal main strip and slit reinforcing strip with two-
point sheet metal barb. Strips are joined by barb passing
around main strip and through opening in the reinforcing
strip. Patented [307005] October 21, 1884, by Francis A.
Blackmer of Springfield, Mass.

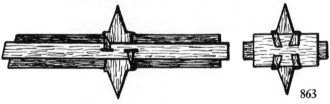

863

Blackmer's Double Strip and Six-lug Barb Lock
Sheet metal main strip and slit reinforcing strip with two-

point sheet metal barb. Barb, mounted between the strips, clips to edges of main strip and through slits in reinforcing strip. Patented [307005] October 21, 1884, by Francis A. Blackmer of Springfield, Mass.

864
Blackmer's Double Strip and Four-lug Barb Lock
Sheet metal main strip and slit reinforcing strip with two-point sheet metal barb. Barb, passing through slits in reinforcing strip, is bent back and clipped to main strip. Patented [307005] October 21, 1884, by Francis A. Blackmer of Springfield, Mass.

865
Blackmer's Double Strip with Blunt-barb, Two-lug Lock
Sheet metal main strip and slit reinforcing strip with two-point sheet metal barb. Lugs on barb pass through slits in reinforcing strip and clip to edges of main strip. Patented [307005] October 21, 1884, by Francis A. Blackmer of Springfield, Mass.

INTEGRATED BARB STRIPS

Extended Points: *Saw Tooth*

Woods' Saw Tooth and Roll   866

Sheet metal strip with one edge serrated and the other rolled into a tube for reinforcement. Patented [214860] April 29, 1879, by Franklin Woods of Allegheny City, Pa.

Woods' Saw Tooth and Half Roll   867

Sheet metal strip with one edge serrated, and the other half rolled for reinforcement. Patented [214860] April 29, 1879, by Franklin Woods of Allegheny City, Pa.

868   Allis' Ribbon, Large Saw-tooth Variation
Sheet metal strip with serrated edge. Prongs run three to the
inch. Variation of patent 244726.

869   Allis' Ribbon, Small Saw-tooth Variation
Reinforced sheet metal strip with serrated edge. Prongs run
five to the inch. Variation of patent 244726.

870   Milligan's Scrap Metal Fencing, Quadrant Cut
Concave sheet metal scraps folded and riveted to form a
barbed cable. Patented [268263] November 28, 1882, by
John C. Milligan of Brooklyn, N.Y.

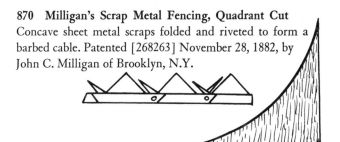

Upham's Barb Strip 871

Sheet metal strip with barbed edge. After strip is cut, barb points are bent to rest against strip and point outward. Patented [272923] February 27, 1883, by Andrew J. Upham of Sycamore, Ill.

Extended Points: *Double Saw Tooth*

Double Serrated-edge Metallic Strip 872

Sheet metal strip with serrated edges. Teeth along the edges point in opposite directions. Designer of fencing strip is unknown.

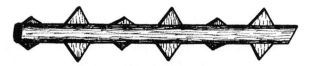

Bate's Strip, Spaced Matching Points 873

Single-strand oval strip with extended triangle-shaped points. Alternately matching points bend in opposite directions. Patented [254904] March 14, 1882, by William S. Bate of Brooklyn, N.Y.

Bate's Strip, Spaced Zigzag Points 874

Single-strand oval strip with extended triangle-shaped points.

Alternately and diagonally matching points bend in opposite directions. Patented [254904] March 14, 1882, by William S. Bate of Brooklyn, N.Y.

875   Bate's Strip, Matching Points
Single-strand oval strip with extended triangle-shaped points. Alternately matching points bend in opposite directions. Patented [254904] March 14, 1882, by William S. Bate of Brooklyn, N.Y.

876   Bate's Strip, Zigzag Points
Single-strand oval strip with extended triangle-shaped points. Alternately and diagonally matching points bend in opposite directions. Patented [254904] March 14, 1882, by William S. Bate of Brooklyn, N.Y.

877   Bate's Strip, Double Saw-tooth Variation
Twisted sheet metal strip with serrated edges. Strip is reinforced with center core. Variation of patent 254904.

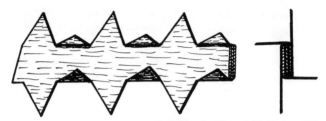

Salisbury's Threefold Strip 878

Folded sheet metal barbed strip. Opposed barbs point in opposite directions. Patented [272482] February 20, 1883, by Charles H. Salisbury, of De Kalb, Ill.

Brock's Folded Saw Tooth 879

Sheet metal strip with serrated edges. Metallic strip has central fold for reinforcement. Patented [294963] February 12, 1884, by William E. Brock of New York, N.Y.

Extended Points: *Cut Edge*

Judson's Serrated Rail 880

Sheet metal strip with projecting spurs. Patented [118135] August 15, 1871, by Lyman P. Judson of Rose, N.Y.

881   Haish's Barbed Rail
Sheet metal strip with cutout barbs along one edge. Strip is reinforced with a center core. Patented [152368] June 23, 1874, by Jacob Haish of De Kalb, Ill.

882   Barnes' Fluted Ribbon
Sheet metal strip with staggered cutout barb points along the edges. Strip is reinforced with center channel. Patented [191913] June 12, 1877, by Walter G. Barnes of Freeport, Ill.

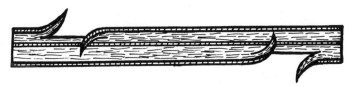

883   Harbaugh's Torn Ribbon
Sheet metal strip ribbed on one side. Paired cutout barbs run along edges. Patented [242636] June 7, 1881, by Joseph W. Harbaugh of Lawrence, Kans.

Brock's Folded Metallic Strip   884

Sheet metal strip with cutout barbs. Metal strip is folded two
times leaving barbs pointed outward at right angles. Patented
[255762] April 4, 1882, by William E. Brock of New York,
N.Y.

885
Ford's Straight-cut Ribbon

Twisted sheet metal strip with cutout barb points along one
edge. Barb points are bent in opposite directions. Patented
[310813] January 13, 1885, by Franklin D. Ford of Providence, R.I.

886
Ford's Bow-cut Ribbon

Twisted sheet metal strip with cutout barb points along one
edge. Barb points are bent in opposite directions. Patented
[310813] January 13, 1885, by Franklin D. Ford of Providence, R.I.

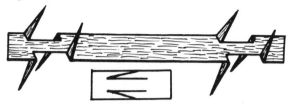

887   Grellner's Four-barb Fence Strip
Sheet metal strip with four barbs cut and formed at regular
intervals. Patented [386742] July 24, 1888, by Christopher J.
Grellner of St. Louis, Mo.

888
Grellner's Corrugated
Four-barb Fence Strip
Corrugated sheet metal strip with four
barbs cut and formed at regular inter-
vals. Patented [386742] July 24, 1888,
by Christopher J. Grellner of St. Louis,
Mo.

889   Grellner's Combination Corrugated
Two- and Four-barb Fence Strip
Corrugated sheet metal strip with six barbs cut and formed at
regular intervals. Patented [386742] July 24, 1888, by Christopher J. Grellner of St. Louis, Mo.

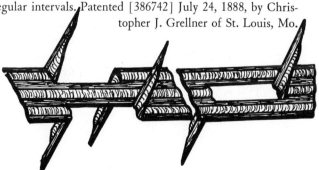

890
Grellner's Corrugated Four-barb Fence Strip,
Diagonal Barb Depressions

Corrugated sheet metal strip with four barbs cut and formed
at regular intervals. Patented [386742] July 24, 1888, by
Christopher J. Grellner of St. Louis, Mo.

891
Grellner's Corrugated Offset Twin-barb Fence Strip,
Diagonal Barb Depressions

Corrugated sheet metal strip with four barbs cut and formed
at regular intervals. Patented [386742] July 24, 1888, by
Christopher J. Grellner of St. Louis, Mo.

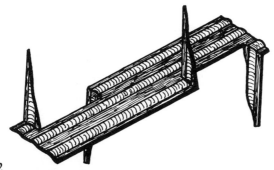

892
Grellner's Corrugated Offset Twin-barb Fence Strip
Corrugated sheet metal strip with four barbs cut and formed
at regular intervals. Patented [386742] July 24, 1888, by
Christopher J. Grellner of St. Louis, Mo.

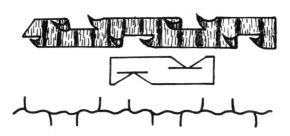

893   **Allis' Corrugated Barb Strip**
Corrugated sheet metal strip with projecting barb points.
Paired barbs bend in opposite directions. Patented [466744]
January 5, 1892, by Thomas V. Allis of New York, N.Y.

Extended Points: *Punch Out*

Clark's Flat Rail   894

Ribbed sheet metal strip with punch-out barbs. Barbs are pressed out in alternate directions along channel. Patented [179268] June 27, 1876, by Norman Clark of Sterling, Ill.

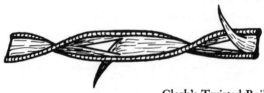

Clark's Twisted Rail   895

Ribbed sheet metal strip with punch-out barbs. Barbs are pressed out in alternate directions along channel. Patented [179268] June 27, 1876, by Norman Clark of Sterling, Ill.

Brink's Strip with Punch-out Barbs   896

Sheet metal strip with punch-out barbs. Patented [183531] October 24, 1876, by Jacob Brinkerhoff of Auburn, N.Y.

897 Brink's Vented Ribbon

Sheet metal perforated strip with punch-out barbs. Barbs point in opposite directions. Patented [186922] February 6, 1877, by Jacob Brinkerhoff of Auburn, N.Y.

898 Nellis' Rail

Fluted sheet metal strip with diagonally-aligned, punch-out barbs. Patented [187723] February 27, 1877, by Aaron J. Nellis of Pittsburgh, Pa.

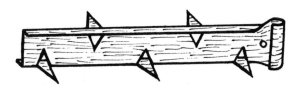

899 Marshall's Rail

Beam-shaped sheet metal strip with punch-out barbs. Patented [244274] July 12, 1881, by Charles K. Marshall of Vicksburg, Miss.

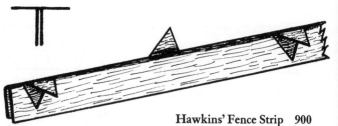

Hawkins' Fence Strip   900

Folded sheet metal strip with cutout barb points. Points extend at right angles to the strip. Patented [307940] November 11, 1884, by Elbert E. Hawkins of Wilkes-Barre, Pa.

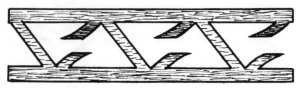

Kilmer's Barbed-window Strip   901

Ornamental sheet metal strip with one leg of opening cut to form barbs. Points bend in opposite directions. Patented [317799] May 12, 1885, by Irving A. and Melvin D. Kilmer of Schenectady, N.Y.

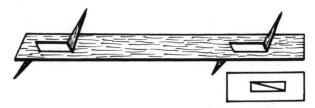

Grellner's Twin-barb Fence Strip   902

Sheet metal strip with twin barbs cut and formed at regular intervals. Patented [386742] July 24, 1888, by Christopher J. Grellner of St. Louis, Mo.

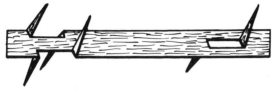

**903 Grellner's Combination Two-
and Four-barb Fence Strip**
Sheet metal strip with six barbs cut and formed at regular
intervals. Patented [386742] July 24, 1888, by Christopher J.
Grellner of St. Louis, Mo.

904 Grellner's Twisted Two-barb Fence Strip
Twisted sheet metal strip with twin barbs cut and formed at
regular intervals. Patented [386742] July 24, 1888, by Christopher J. Grellner of St. Louis, Mo.

905 Grellner's Corrugated Two-barb Fence Strip
Corrugated sheet metal strip with twin barbs cut and formed
at regular intervals. Patented [386742] July 24, 1888, by
Christopher J. Grellner of St. Louis, Mo.

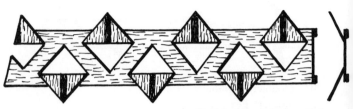

Perkins' Barb Strip   906

Sheet metal strip with staggered punch-out barb points. Edges
of strip are folded for reinforcement. Patented [478170] July
5, 1892, by Richard B. Perkins of Hornellsville, N.Y.

Dent's Barbed Strip   907

Sheet metal strip with paired punch-out prongs. Points are
turned under to reduce injury to stock. Patented [578447]
March 9, 1897, by Samuel Dent of Jansville, Idaho.

Extended Points: *Prong*

Allis' Buckthorn   908

Sheet metal strip with lance points and large reinforcing
central core. Patented [244726] July 26, 1881, by Thomas V.
Allis of New York, N.Y.

909   Allis' Buckthorn, Narrow-strip Variation
Sheet metal strip with lance points and small reinforcing
central core. Variation of patent 244726.

910   Allis' Buckthorn, Wide-strip Variation
Sheet metal strip with lance points and small reinforcing
central core. Variation of patent 244726.

911   Allis' Buckthorn Ribbon, Square-rib Variation
Sheet metal strip with off-center, rectangular reinforcing rib.
Variation of patent 244726.

Allis' Buckthorn, Receding Points Variation   912

Sheet metal strip with lance points and reinforcing central core. Large points are separated by series of small points. Variation of patent 244726.

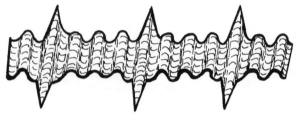

Gregg's Corrugated Barb Strip   913

Corrugated sheet metal strip with prongs extending outward along the edges. Patented [258412] May 23, 1882, by Samuel H. Gregg of Crawfordsville, Ind.

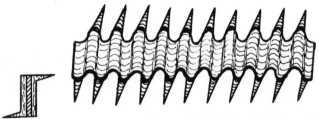

Carpenter's Stickered Ribbon   914

Corrugated sheet metal strip with extended prongs along edges. Prongs are bent at right angles to strip and in opposite directions from edges. Patented [258887] June 6, 1882, by James Carpenter of Moravia, N.Y.

915   Carpenter's Serpent Wire
Oval undulating wire with laterally extended prongs. Patented
[258888] June 6, 1882, by James Carpenter of Moravia, N.Y.

916   Allis' Barbed Half Round
Single-strand, half-round metallic fencing with barb points
extending out from the core, or body. Patented [266336]
September 19, 1882, by Thomas V. Allis of New York, N.Y.

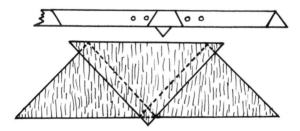

917   Milligan's Scrap Metal Fencing, Triangle Cut
Overlapping sheet metal scraps folded and riveted to form a
barbed cable. Patented [268263] November 28, 1882, by John
C. Milligan of Brooklyn, N.Y.

Brock's Crimped Ribbon   918

Sheet metal strip with extended barb points. Strip is reinforced with a crimped ridge through the center. Patented
[293411] February 12, 1884, by William E. Brock of New
York, N.Y.

Kelly's Metallic Spurs   919

Sheet metal strip with projecting points. Points along one
edge are bent in the opposite direction from those on the
other. Center flute reinforces strip. Patented [296753] April
15, 1884, by John E. Kelly of Fryeburg, Maine.

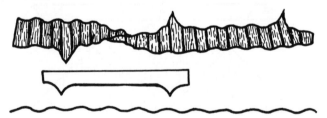

Allis' Corrugated Twist Strip   920

Twisted corrugated sheet metal strip with extended barb
points along one edge. Patented [466746] January 5, 1892, by
Thomas V. Allis of New York, N.Y.

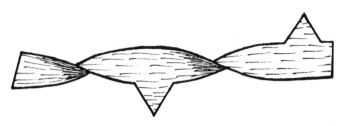

921   Allis' Strip, Plain Strip Variation
Sheet metal strip with projecting barb points along one edge.
Variation of patent 466746.

922   Allis' Black Hills Ribbon
Twisted sheet metal strip with alternating lance and cutout
barbs. Cutout barb points bend in opposite directions. Patented
[501129] July 11, 1893, by Thomas V. Allis of New York,
N.Y.

923   Allis' Sunken Lance Ribbon
Twisted sheet metal strip with projecting barbs along one
edge. Base of barb set below edge. Patented [538401] April
30, 1895, by Thomas V. Allis of New York, N.Y.

Allis' Buckthorn, Modern Plastic Variation 924

Plastic strip with projecting prongs along edges. Strip is reinforced by two longitudinal steel wires. Variation of patent 244726.

Extended Points: *Segmented Edge*

Mann's Spiny Rail 925

Sheet metal strip with projecting spines. Spines and supports are cut and folded from the same stock. Patented [276439] April 24, 1883, by Charles A. Mann of Buffalo, N.Y.

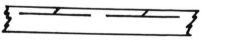

**926
Jordan's Ribbon,
Segmented Edge**

Twisted sheet metal strip with one edge cut in segments to form barbs. Patented [301126] July 1, 1884, by Edmund Jordan of Brooklyn, N.Y.

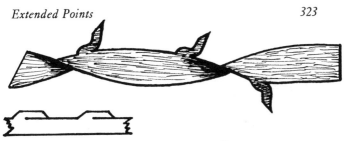

927 Jordan's Metallic Strip, Spaced Half Segments
Twisted sheet metal strip with spaced half segments along one edge. Patented [302534] July 22, 1884, by Edmund Jordan of Brooklyn, N.Y.

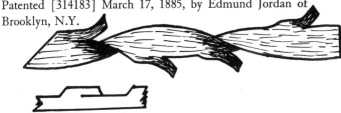

928 Jordan's Metallic Strip, Spaced Segments
Twisted sheet metal strip with spaced segments along one edge. Patented [302534] July 22, 1884, by Edmund Jordan of Brooklyn, N.Y.

929 Jordan's Strip, Straight-cut Segment
Twisted sheet metal strip with barb segments along one edge. Patented [314183] March 17, 1885, by Edmund Jordan of Brooklyn, N.Y.

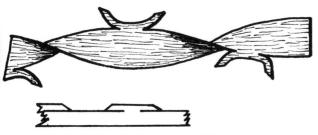

930
Jordan's Strip, Slant-cut Segment
Twisted sheet metal strip with barb segments along one edge.
Patented [314183] March 17, 1885, by Edmund Jordan of
Brooklyn, N.Y.

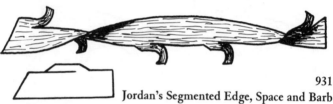

931
Jordan's Segmented Edge, Space and Barb
Twisted sheet metal strip with spaced segments along one
edge extending outward to form barbs. Patented [444957]
January 20, 1891, by Edmund Jordan of Brooklyn, N.Y.

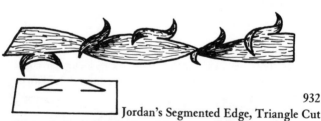

932
Jordan's Segmented Edge, Triangle Cut
Twisted sheet metal strip with segments along one edge extending outward to form barbs. Patented [444957] January
20, 1891, by Edmund Jordan of Brooklyn, N.Y.

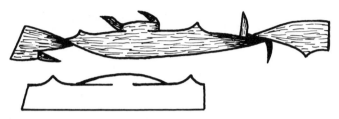

933 Allis' Segmented Edge, Dome Cut
Twisted sheet metal strip with segments along one edge extending outward to form barbs. Patented [446557] February 17, 1891, by Thomas V. Allis of New York, N.Y.

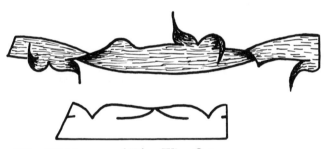

934 Allis' Segmented Edge, Wing Cut
Twisted sheet metal strip with segments along one edge extending outward to form barbs. Cutaway along edge of strip leaves two pointed and one round projection alternately. Patented [446558] February 17, 1891, by Thomas V. Allis of New York, N.Y.

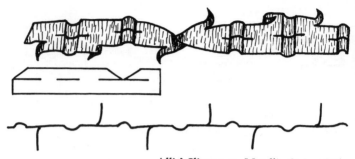

Allis' Slit-groove Metallic Strip   935
Twisted and grooved sheet metal strip with segmented barb
points along both edges. Patented [466745] January 5, 1892,
by Thomas V. Allis of New York, N.Y.

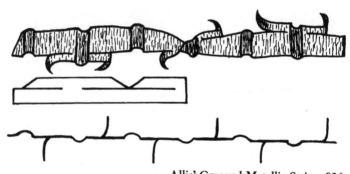

Allis' Grooved Metallic Strip   936
Twisted and grooved sheet metal strip with segmented barb
points along both edges. Patented [466747] January 5, 1892,
by Thomas V. Allis of New York, N.Y.

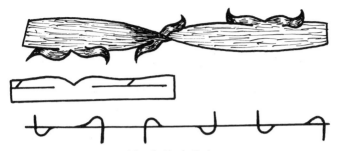

937 Allis' Segmented-hook Barb Strip
Twisted sheet metal strip with segmented edges. Segments are bent to form hook barbs. Patented [466748] January 5, 1892, by Thomas V. Allis of New York, N.Y.

Extended Points: *Knife-Edge*

938 Connelly's Knife-edge Ribbon
Sheet metal strip with knife-edges. Patented [254278] February 28, 1882, by Joseph H. Connelly of Pittsburgh, Pa.

Extended Points: *Split Panel*

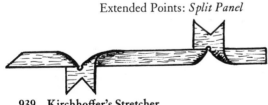

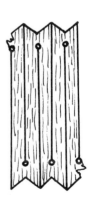

939 Kirchhoffer's Stretcher
Sheet metal strip cut and stretched to form strand and two-point barbs. Patented [238296] March 1, 1881, by George W. Kirchhoffer of Chicago, Ill.

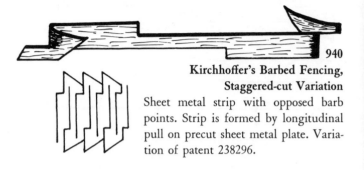

940

Kirchhoffer's Barbed Fencing, Staggered-cut Variation

Sheet metal strip with opposed barb points. Strip is formed by longitudinal pull on precut sheet metal plate. Variation of patent 238296.

Extruded Points: *Rod*

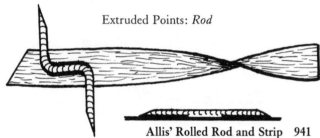

Allis' Rolled Rod and Strip   941

Sheet metal strip and rod-shaped barb rolled from the same stock. Rod is partly cut from strip to permit bending at each end to form barb points. Patented [272933] February 27, 1883, by Thomas V. Allis of New York, N.Y.

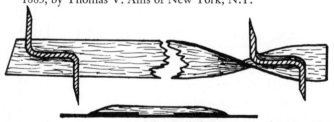

Allis' Rolled Segment and Strip   942

Sheet metal strip and two-point, crescent-shaped barb. Barb and strip are rolled from the same stock. Ends of segment are partly cut from strip and bent to form the barb points. Patented [272936] February 27, 1883, by Thomas V. Allis of New York, N.Y.

Extruded Points: *Knob*

943 Howell's Pyramid-knob Fence Rod
Twisted metallic rod with knobbed surfaces. Knobs and rod are formed from the same material. Patented [299072] May 20, 1884, by William G. Howell of Philadelphia, Pa.

944 Howell's Round-knob Fence Rod
Twisted metallic rod with knobbed surfaces. Knobs and rod are formed from the same material. Patented [299072] May 20, 1884, by William G. Howell of Philadelphia, Pa.

945 Roop's Fencing Strip
Ribbed metallic strip with extended barbs and square projections. Patented [345259] July 6, 1886, by Jacob Warren Roop of Harrisburg, Pa.

Section III. Bars, Rods, Wooden Rails

Bars, rods, and wooden rails were included among the various types of fencing shipped to the western prairies. Although equipped with prongs or spikes, there was little else to distinguish this improved fencing from the traditional wooden rails. Well constructed, it had the appearance of substantiality and strength not apparent in wire and metallic strip fencing, making it seem a more effective barrier for livestock.

It had more tangible advantages, however. It was clearly visible to animals, was not subject to stretching, could be dismantled quickly to allow passage of livestock or vehicle and could be bundled and stacked conveniently for storage and transportation.

Except for small enclosures, neither bar, rod, nor rail fencing was widely used in the prairies and plains of the western states. It was too expensive. When compared to the more conventional wire and metallic strip fencing, it required more time to erect, called for a greater amount of material, and presented transportation problems because of its bulk.

BARS

Prong

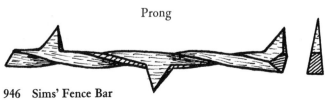

946 Sims' Fence Bar

Triangular-shaped bar and lance barbs. Barbs are cut from a
ridge in the original material. Patented [178195] May 30,
1876, by Elijah Sims of Aurora, Ill.

947 Allis' Fence Bar

Square iron bar with projecting lance barbs along one edge.
Patented [209790] November 12, 1878, by Thomas V. Allis
of New York, N.Y.

Serrated Edge

948 Connelly's Knife-edge V-Bar

Metallic V-shaped iron rail with knife-edges. Patented
[247537] September 27, 1881, by Joseph H. Connelly of Allegheny, Pa.

Connelly's Knife-edge T-Bar   949

Metallic T-shaped iron rail with knife-edges. Patented
[247537] September 27, 1881, by Joseph H. Connelly of Allegheny, Pa.

Connelly's Knife-edge Crossbar   950

Metallic cross-shaped iron rail with knife-edges. Patented
[247537] September 27, 1881, by Joseph H. Connelly of
Allegheny, Pa.

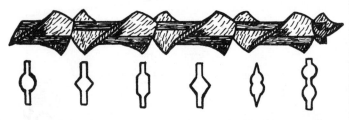

Schmidt's Fence Strip   951

Metallic strips of various shapes die-cut to form successive
barbs along edges. Patented [368014] August 9, 1887, by
Julius Schmidt of Hagen, Westphalia, Prussia, Ger.

952   Beresford's Serrated Triangle Fence Rod
Triangle-shaped iron rod with saw-tooth edge. Patented
[449279] March 31, 1891, by James Beresford of Manchester,
Eng.

RODS

Insert

Randall's Rod   953

Metal rod with two-point metal pegs inserted at right angles to each other along the body. T-shaped head of rod fits into brackets in steel posts. Patented [359178] March 8, 1887, by Benjamin F. Randall of Fall River, Mass.

Knife-Edge

Beresford Triangle Fence Rod   954

Triangle-shaped iron rod with dull knife-edges. Patented [449279] March 31, 1891, by James Beresford of Manchester, Eng.

Extruded Points

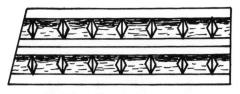

955 Perry's Four-edge Grooved Rail
Grooved iron rail with dull edges and multiple circular projections. Patented [333887] January 5, 1886, by W. H. Perry of Sharon, Pa.

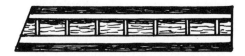

956 Perry's Blunt-edge Grooved Rail
Grooved iron rail with deterrent crossribbing. Patented [333887] January 5, 1886, by W. H. Perry of Sharon, Pa.

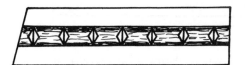

957 Perry's Knife-edge Grooved Rail
Grooved iron rail with dull edges and multiple projecting points. Patented [333887] January 5, 1886, by W. H. Perry of Sharon, Pa.

WOODEN RAILS

Insert

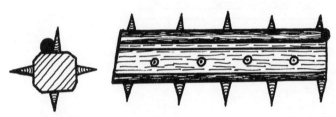

Rose's Rail   958

Wooden rail supported by an iron rod. Sharpened pieces of wire are inserted in wooden rail to form points. Patented [138763] May 13, 1873, by Henry M. Rose of Waterman Station, Ill.

Richards' Protectors   959

Shaped spikes driven into board rail at staggered intervals. A special tool is used for forcing the large end of spike into the board. Patented [191468] May 29, 1877, by Marcius C. Richards of Oswego, Ill.

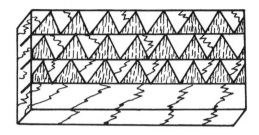

960 Topliff's Barrier

Grooved wooden strip armed with serrated metallic strips. Assembled barrier is fastened along top of fence. Patented [191818] June 12, 1877, by Cyrus L. Topliff of Brooklyn, N.Y.

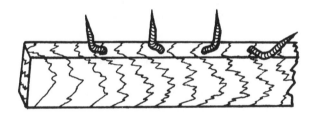

961 Housum's Rail and Bent Barb

Wooden rail with single-point wire barbs driven into one edge. Wire barbs are cut and shaped with hand tool. Patented [204735] June 11, 1878, by Charles P. Housum of Decatur, Ill.

Housum's Rail and Arched Barb   962

Wooden rail with single-point barb driven into one edge. Wire barbs are cut and shaped with hand tool. Patented [204735] June 11, 1878, by Charles P. Housum of Decatur, Ill.

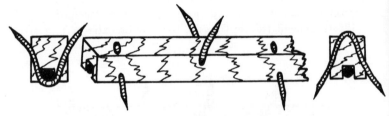

Walsh–Dutol's Barbed Rail   963

Grooved wooden rail, reinforcing rod, and staple barb. Rail and rod are held together with alternate barbs. Patented [223780] January 20, 1880, by John Walsh and James Dutol of Newton, Iowa.

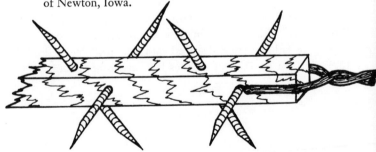

Orwig's Barbed Rail   964

Wooden rail with wire-barb inserts. Rails connect to each

other and to posts with twisted strands of wire. Patented [225717] March 23, 1880, by Thomas G. Orwig of Des Moines, Iowa.

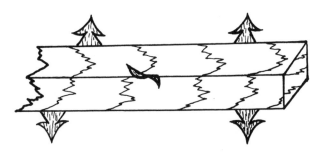 

965 Chapman's Barbed Rail
Wooden rail with three-point brad barbs. Barbs are staggered along edges of rail at a forty-five degree angle. Patented [246866] September 13, 1881, by Melville S. Chapman of Elkhart, Ind.

Barb

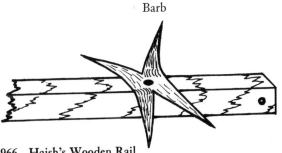

966 Haish's Wooden Rail
Wooden rail with four-prong sheet metal barb plate. Barb plate is nailed to the rail. Patented [147634] February 17, 1874, by Jacob Haish of De Kalb, Ill.

Section IV. Pickets

Picket fencing held little promise as an effective barrier to livestock in the western plains and prairies because of the limitations of cost. It was too expensive to manufacture, to produce in quantity, and to erect on a scale that would enable it to compete with wire and metallic strip fencing.

Pickets consisted of spikes, slats, or a combination of both. Picket fencing was ornamental, strong, often rigid, and quite visible to animals. Spikes installed along the top of board or stone fences prevented intruders from scaling or climbing over them. When slats were used in fencing, they were closely spaced between twisted strands of wire or fastened to board rails. There was small chance of livestock being injured except where the slats were equipped with metallic points or spurs.

PICKETS

Spikes

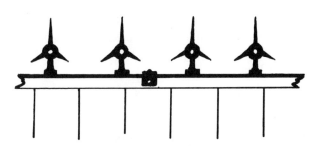

967 Dabb's Picketed Strip
Sheet metal strip with fixed iron spikes running along top of
fence. Patented [63482] April 2, 1867, by Alphonso Dabb of
Elizabethport, N.J.

968 Dabb's Picketed Strip
Sheet metal strip with fixed iron spikes running along top of
fence. Patented [63482] April 2, 1867, by Alphonso Dabb of
Elizabethport, N.J.

Dabb's Picketed Strip   969

Sheet metal strip with fixed iron spikes running along top of
fence. Patented [63482] April 2, 1867, by Alphonso Dabb of
Elizabethport, N.J.

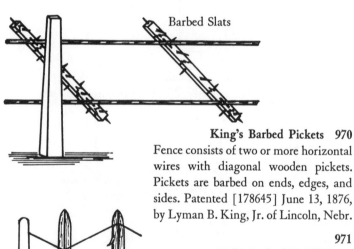

Barbed Slats

King's Barbed Pickets   970

Fence consists of two or more horizontal
wires with diagonal wooden pickets.
Pickets are barbed on ends, edges, and
sides. Patented [178645] June 13, 1876,
by Lyman B. King, Jr. of Lincoln, Nebr.

971

Fish's Barbed Picket Fence

Picket fence of truss wires and T-angle
iron pickets. Center rib of picket is
notched for truss wires and the outer
edges slit to form barbs. Patented
[218373] August 12, 1879, by George
M. Fish of Chicago, Ill.

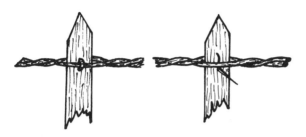

972 Bernard–Rice's Interwoven Picket

Combination two-strand wire and interwoven pickets. Common staple serves for fastener and barb. Patented [243835] July 5, 1881, by David B. Bernard and Elisha H. Rice of Kirksville, Mo.

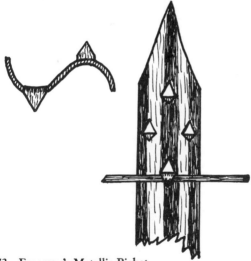

973 Emerson's Metallic Picket

Fluted sheet metal picket with punch-out barb points. Patented [358602] March 1, 1887, by James E. Emerson of Beaver Falls, Pa.

Section V. Warning Devices

Erecting an effective barrier against straying livestock was the desire of ranchers and farmers alike, and they were concerned that a barrier should restrain but not injure an animal. Consequently, various warning devices were developed to enable tractable animals to discover the existence of barbed wire fences before they were cut or crippled. These devices were attached to the wire at the factory or later when the wire was stretched for fencing.

Warning devices bore such names as "barbed wire signals," "indicators," "warning strips," "warning plates," and "cattle protectors." Made of paper, wood, or metal, they appeared in the shapes of tags, plates, blocks, balls, strips, and slats. The strips and slats also served as fence stays and spacers.

After it was learned that livestock soon became conditioned to the presence of barbed wire fences and stayed clear of them, warning devices completely lost what little prominence they had previously gained.

WARNING DEVICES

Plates

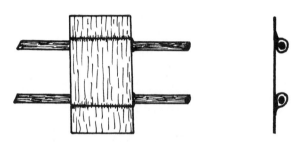

974 Briggs' Tin Plate
Parallel single-wire strands with crimped-on sheet metal plate. Seams are off-center to strands. Patented [252071] January 10, 1882, by Orlando P. Briggs of Chicago, Ill.

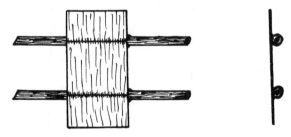

975 Briggs' Center-seam Tin Plate
Parallel single-wire strands with crimped-on sheet metal plate. Seams are centered on the strands. Patented [252071] January 10, 1882, by Orlando P. Briggs of Chicago, Ill.

Sergeant's Warning Plate   976

Two-strand wire with sheet metal plate. Supports bend in opposite directions to hold plate in place. Patented [299169] May 27, 1884, by Raphael Sergeant of Pittsburgh, Pa.

Gholson's Warning Plate   977

Two parallel double strands with sheet metal warning plate. Patented [353129] November 23, 1886, by William C. Gholson of Cincinnati, Ohio.

Strips

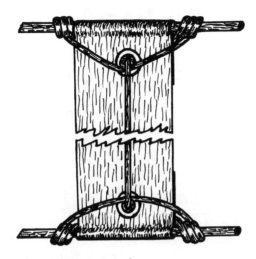

978   Hoisington Fence Guard
Perforated sheet metal strip with wire tie. Strip is fastened
vertically and at staggered intervals in fencing. Inventor of
device is unknown.

979   Crandal's Indicator
Sheet metal plate bent to slip down over fence strands. A
wooden block is inserted in the device to rest on the wire.
Lower bend in plate prevents indicator dropping off. Patented
[220912] October 28, 1879, by Edward M. Crandal of Chicago,
Ill.

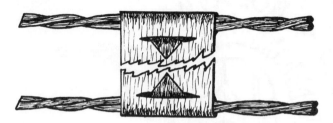

Bentley's Indicator   980

Sheet metal strap with slot-and-tongue fasteners. Straps are staggered in fencing. Patented [300940] June 24, 1884, by Charles S. Bentley of Dubuque, Iowa.

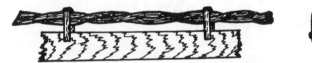

Pratt's Warning Strip   981

Wooden rail suspended with metal straps from fence wire. One end of strap is bolted to rail. Spring action of other end permits easy mounting. Patented [348929] September 7, 1886, by H. C. Pratt of Canandagua, N.Y.

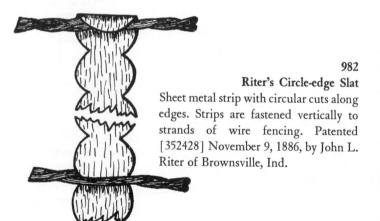

982
Riter's Circle-edge Slat

Sheet metal strip with circular cuts along edges. Strips are fastened vertically to strands of wire fencing. Patented [352428] November 9, 1886, by John L. Riter of Brownsville, Ind.

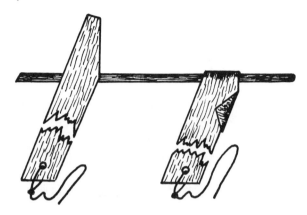

983 Raile's Fence Signal
Sheet metal strip folded and crimped to one fence wire and
anchored to another with a tie wire. Patented [367664]
August 2, 1887, by Robert E. Raile of Topeka, Kans.

Blocks

984 Boone's Round Guard Block
Round block adaptable to either wire or metallic strip. Sheet
metal insert holds guard in place. Patented [294572] March 4,
1884, by Robert Boone, Jr. of Philadelphia, Pa.

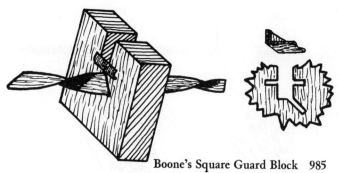

Boone's Square Guard Block   985

Square block adaptable to either wire or metallic strip. Sheet metal insert holds guard in place. Patented [294572] March 4, 1884, by Robert Boone, Jr. of Philadelphia, Pa.

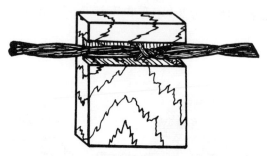

Boone's Side-slot Visible Guard   986

Perforated wooden block with slot cut in one side to receive the wire strands. Tie wire holds block in place on the strands. Patented [321787] July 7, 1885, by Robert Boone, Jr. of Philadelphia, Pa.

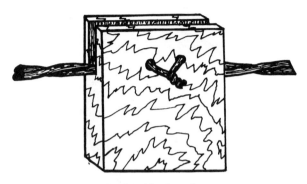

987   Boone's Top-slot Visible Guard

Perforated wooden block with slot cut in one end to receive wire strands. Tie wire above strands holds block in place. Patented [321787] July 7, 1885, by Robert Boone, Jr. of Philadelphia, Pa.

988   Chappell's Wire Guard

T-shaped suspension block for fence strand. Tie wire is crimped after passing around strand and through a hole in the block. Patented [401133] April 9, 1889, by Merritt B. Chappell of Battle Creek, Iowa.

Balls

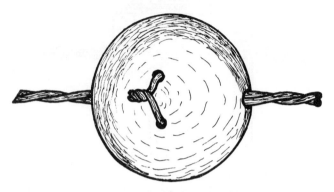

Bacon's Wire-fastened Warning Ball   989
Wooden ball with hole through center. Ball is cut in half.
Halves are mounted on fence strands and tied together with
wire through off-center holes. Patented [297487] April 22,
1884, by Charles H. Bacon of Springfield, Ohio.

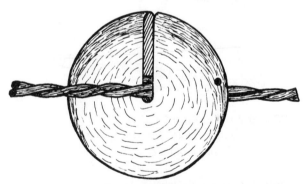

Bacon's Pin-fastened Warning Ball   990
Wooden ball with opening cut past the center. Ball is mounted
on fence and held in place with wire pin. Patented [297487]
April 22, 1884, by Charles H. Bacon of Springfield, Ohio.

Tags

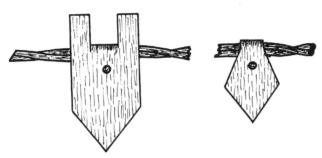

991   Schlyer's Fence Signal
Paired sheet metal plates riveted to fence strand. Plates are
free to rotate. Patented [405851] June 25, 1889, by John
Schlyer of Hays City, Kans.

992   Herweyer's Warning Plates
Quarter-moon and shield-shaped sheet metal plates. Plates
are suspended alternately along fence wire. Patented [517548]
April 3, 1894, by Leonard Herweyer of Vogel Centre, Mich.

References

1. Government Documents

Official Gazette Issued by the U.S. Patent Office from 1853 to 1897, Inclusive. Department of Commerce, Washington, D.C.

Patent Specifications (Reprints of Wire, and Metallic Strip Fencing Inventions) Issued by the U.S. Patent Office from 1853 to 1897, Inclusive. Department of Commerce, Washington, D.C.

2. Newspapers

The American Barbed Wire Journal (Snyder, Texas), June, 1967–May, 1968.

Barb Wire Times (McAlester, Oklahoma), June, 1967–May, 1968.

3. Books

McCallum, Henry D., and Frances T. *The Wire that Fenced the West.* Norman, University of Oklahoma Press, 1965.

James, Jesse S. *Early United States Barbed Wire Patents.* Maywood, California, Privately Printed (1966).

Webb, Walter Prescott. *The Great Plains.* Boston, Gin and Company, 1931.

4. Periodicals

McClure, C. Boone, editor. "History of the Manufacture of Barbed Wire," *Panhandle-Plains Historical Review* (1958).

Indexes

INDEX TO PATENTS

1876

182212	Sept. 12	McGlin, James C. and Hart, Thomas E.	228
182351	Sept. 19	Brown, Rollin G.	245
182626	Sept. 26	Armstrong, Frank	74, 179
182778	Oct. 3	Vosburgh, Cyrus A.	46, 118, 119
182817	Oct. 3	Gilman, W. H.	285
182819	Oct. 3	Harsha, Mortimer S.	72
182928	Oct. 3	Hill, Peter P.	247
182976	Oct. 3	Weber, Theodore A.	66
183531	Oct. 24	Brinkerhoff, Jacob	312
183552	Oct. 24	Evans, Lemuel E.	246
183883	Oct. 31	Bagger, Louis	67
184486	Nov. 21	Watkins, William	189, 191, 193, 194
184694	Nov. 28	Billings, George W.	150, 224
184844	Nov. 28	Crandal, Edward M.	232, 233
185333	Dec. 12	Knickerbocker, Millis	74
185346	Dec. 12	Nelson, John C.	47
185688	Dec. 26	Merrill, John C.	54, 65, 146

Reissues

| 6913 | Feb. 8 | Glidden, Joseph F. | 30, 31, 98, 99 |
| 6914 | Feb. 8 | Glidden, Joseph F. | 50–53, 145, 254 |

1877

186716	Jan. 30	Decker, Alexander C.	253
186922	Feb. 6	Brinkerhoff, Jacob	313
187049	Feb. 6	Reynolds, William L.	198
187172	Feb. 6	Putman, Henry W.	32
187723	Feb. 27	Nellis, Aaron J.	313
189047	Apr. 3	Kittleson, Ole O.	48
189122	Apr. 3	McNeill, John	124
189861	Apr. 24	Hunt, George G.	233
189994	Apr. 24	Bronson, Adelbert E.	141, 248
190081	Apr. 24	Scarlett, Charles W. and William	78, 79
190167	May 1	Stover, Daniel C.	28
190836	May 15	Dobbs, John	28
191011	May 22	Nellis, Aaron J.	277
191263	May 29	Steward, John F.	248
191348	May 29	Judson, Lyman P.	285
191468	May 29	Richards, Marcius C.	338
191818	June 12	Topliff, Cyrus L.	339
191913	June 12	Barnes, Walter G.	307
191993	June 12	Nellis, Aaron J.	275

206754	Aug. 6	Underwood, Henry M.	213, 231
207710	Sept. 3	Brotherton, Jacob	111–13, 167, 219
208001	Sept. 10	Tysdal, Knud	248, 249
208140	Sept. 17	Baker, Charles H. and	
		Bestor, Francis L.	129, 130
208538	Oct. 1	Pitney, Albert L.	44, 116
208688	Oct. 8	Miles, Purches	28
209467	Oct. 29	Daley, Michael	38, 39, 58
209790	Nov. 12	Allis, Thomas V.	333

1879

211349	Jan. 14	Shuman, Thomas	197
211863	Feb. 4	Parker, Charles P.	185
212080	Feb. 4	Winterbotham, J.	160
212874	Mar. 4	Vaughan, Henry M.	113
214095	Apr. 8	Brinkerhoff, Jacob	277–80
214211	Apr. 8	Wager, William H.	146
214417	Apr. 15	Munson, Andrew M.	61
214860	Apr. 29	Woods, Franklin	302
215404	May 13	Shuman, Thomas	69, 175, 186
215888	May 27	Crowell, J. S.	195
216294	June 10	Ross, Noble G.	152, 153
216358	June 10	Swan, Frank	189
216637	June 17	Wilkes, Edward V.	63
218290	Aug. 5	Lord, Tyler C.	81, 183, 184
218373	Aug. 12	Fish, George M.	346
218506	Aug. 12	Duncan, John A.	61, 160
219067	Sept. 2	Burroughs, Henry R.	296
219143	Sept. 2	Brinkerhoff, Jacob and Warren M.	275, 276
220740	Oct. 21	Weaver, James H.	255
220912	Oct. 20	Crandal, Edward M.	353
221158	Nov. 4	Crandal, Edward M.	208
221300	Nov. 4	Gregg, Samuel H.	136, 170, 182
221427	Nov. 11	Sherman, Charles A.	248, 250
222747	Dec. 16	Stevens, Sidney M.	163

1880

223780	Jan. 20	Welch, John and Dutot, James	340
224482	Feb. 10	Scutt, Hiram B.	142
225717	Mar. 23	Orwig, Thomas G.	340

1881

250219	Nov. 29	Dodge, Thomas H.	82
250899	Dec. 13	Dodge, Thomas H.	77
251273	Dec. 20	Neely, Thomas and Marland, Alfred	87, 212
251276	Dec. 20	Olsen, Olaf R.	82
251505	Dec. 27	Barker, George E.	83, 204

1882

252071	Jan. 10	Briggs, Orlando P.	351
252746	Jan. 24	Dodge, Thomas H. and Washburn, Charles G.	146–48
253022	Jan. 31	Ellwood, Abram	125, 126, 164, 225
253632	Feb. 14	Schmeiser, Henry J.	44
254278	Feb. 28	Connelly, Joseph H.	327
254539	Mar. 7	Decker, Alexander C.	155
254888	Mar. 14	Smallwood, Scott	73, 77
254904	Mar. 14	Bate, William S.	304, 305
254923	Mar. 14	Clark, Norman	220
255399	Mar. 21	Upham, Andrew J.	286
255728	Mar. 28	Evans, Lemuel E.	117, 252
255762	Apr. 4	Brock, William E.	308
255763	Apr. 4	Brock, William E.	86
256535	Apr. 18	Baker, George C.	270
256880	Apr. 25	Case, George	47
257196	May 2	Wiles, Robert H.	121
258014	May 16	Brinkerhoff, Jacob and Warren M.	69, 168
258412	May 23	Gregg, Samuel H.	318
258706	May 30	Brinkerhoff, Jacob and Warren M.	75, 177
258887	June 6	Carpenter, James	318
258888	June 6	Carpenter, James	319
258914	June 6	Harris, William M.	286
260268	June 27	Wiles, Robert H.	134
260844	July 11	Clark, Norman	213, 214
261185	July 18	Upham, Andrew J.	155, 163
261212	July 18	Elsey, George	186, 187
261619	July 25	Massey, Ward E.	265
261703	July 25	Haish, Jacob	29
261704	July 25	Haish, Jacob	172, 173
262200	Aug. 8	Bodman, Charles G.	163, 164
264110	Sept. 12	Scutt, John F.	190
264436	Sept. 19	Brainerd, Frank W.	135
264495	Sept. 19	Upham, Andrew J.	121

281300	July 17	Root, William A.	165
282449	July 31	Dodge, Thomas H.	107, 108
282453	July 31	Goss, Joseph	205
283614	Aug. 21	Kelly, Michael	91, 287
284218	Sept. 4	Mann, Charles A.	271
284261	Sept. 4	Upham, Andrew J.	32, 33, 108
285014	Sept. 18	Clow, William M.	131
285229	Sept. 18	Childs, J. Wallace	298, 299
286130	Oct. 2	Gunderson, Albert	156
286147	Oct. 2	Oliver, James B.	193, 195
286507	Oct. 9	Upham, Andrew J.	138
286512	Oct. 9	Weber, Theodore A.	117
286987	Oct. 16	Kay, William V.	240
287059	Oct. 23	Scutt, Hiram B.	282
287091	Oct. 23	Brainard, Curtis B.	195
287261	Oct. 23	Evans, John Elias	206, 231
287337	Oct. 23	Stubbe, John	199
287372	Oct. 23	Ford, John C.	188, 200
287391	Oct. 23	Reynolds, William R.	11
287803	Nov. 6	Clow, William M.	131
289076	Nov. 27	Dodge, Thomas H.	177
289207	Nov. 27	Barr, Charles H.	174, 188, 200
290974	Dec. 25	Cline, John B.	224

1884

291420	Jan. 1	Stevens, Amasa W.	45
293411	Feb. 12	Brock, William E.	320
293412	Feb. 12	Brock, William E.	11, 30
293584	Feb. 12	Lord, Tyler C.	166
294572	Mar. 4	Boone, Jr., Robert	355, 356
294612	Mar. 4	Gore, Willis K.	227
294827	Mar. 11	Upham, Andrew J.	173
294963	Mar. 11	Brock, William E.	306
296060	Apr. 1	Potts, Albert	276
296753	Apr. 15	Kelly, John E.	320
296835	Apr. 15	Hulbert, Arthur G.	89, 142
297203	Apr. 22	Underwood, Henry M.	143
297487	Apr. 22	Bacon, Charles H.	358
298193	May 6	Forrester, Samuel	201, 202
298440	May 13	Brainard, Curtis B.	70, 168
299072	May 20	Howell, William G.	329

319807	June 9	Ford, Franklin D.	272, 273
321264	June 30	Wheeler, Elonzo S.	199
321787	July 7	Boone, Jr., Robert	356, 357
322108	July 14	Kelly, Michael	45, 73, 117, 220
323724	Aug. 4	Pattison, George H.	135
324221	Aug. 11	Brinkerhoff, John J.	273–75
327755	Oct. 6	Beerbower, George M.	139
330893	Nov. 24	Hill, Christian C.	122
330993	Nov. 24	Matteson, Eugene R.	139
331908	Dec. 8	Potter, James	118
332252	Dec. 15	Haish, Jacob	176
332393	Dec. 15	Haish, Jacob	289, 294
332755	Dec. 22	Scutt, Hiram B.	123, 171

1886

333887	Jan. 5	Perry, W. H.	337
336664	Feb. 23	Potter, James	118
338229	Mar. 16	Hunt, J. E.	43
341921	May 18	Kraft, Charles J. F. and Augustus, C. H.	43, 123
343482	June 8	McGill, George W.	240, 242, 243
344077	June 22	Brock, Adaline	269
344428	June 29	Whitney, Jack F. and Hubbell, Myron R.	244
345259	July 6	Roop, Jacob W.	329
348929	Sept. 7	Pratt, H. C.	354
352428	Nov. 9	Riter, John L.	209, 210, 354
353129	Nov. 23	Gholson, William C.	352

1887

356762	Feb. 1	Haish, Jacob	33, 34, 93
358602	Mar. 1	Emerson, James E.	347
359178	Mar. 8	Randall, Benjamin F.	336
367398	Aug. 2	Hodge, Chester A.	206, 207
367664	Aug. 2	Raile, Robert E.	355
367893	Aug. 9	Cloud, William J.	210
368014	Aug. 9	Schmidt, Julius	334
369825	Sept. 13	Utter, Homer	212
373772	Nov. 22	Fisher, Jr., George P.	296, 297

1888

1889

1890

1891

465391	Dec. 15	Shellaberger, M. M.	12, 13
465629	Dec. 22	Lewis, Elliott L.	234
465630	Dec. 22	Lewis, Elliott L.	234
465638	Dec. 22	Griswold, John Wool	234
465639	Dec. 22	Griswold, John Wool	235
465640	Dec. 22	Griswold, John Wool	235
465641	Dec. 22	Griswold, John Wool	235
465642	Dec. 22	Griswold, John Wool	236
465643	Dec. 22	Griswold, John Wool	236
465644	Dec. 22	Griswold, John Wool	236
465645	Dec. 22	Griswold, John Wool	237

1892

466744	Jan. 5	Allis, Thomas V.	311
466745	Jan. 5	Allis, Thomas V.	326
466746	Jan. 5	Allis, Thomas V.	320, 321
466747	Jan. 5	Allis, Thomas V.	326
466748	Jan. 5	Allis, Thomas V.	327
466775	Jan. 12	Deines, George	68
469062	Feb. 16	Ingraham, T. J.	18, 230
470746	Mar. 16	Curtis, John D.	94, 95, 251
470747	Mar. 15	Curtis, John D.	95
472044	Apr. 5	Gearty, Hugh	211
472496	Apr. 5	Griswold, John Wool	237
475718	May 24	Cleaveland, John B.	19, 20
475719	May 24	Cleaveland, John B.	20
478170	July 5	Perkins, Richard B.	267, 316
484890	Oct. 25	Curtis, John D.	166
486173	Nov. 15	Allis, Thomas V.	266
486179	Nov. 15	Griswold, John Wool	241
486824	Nov. 22	Cleaveland, John B.	13

1893

490187	Jan. 17	Delffs, Arnold	68, 167
493210	Mar. 7	Funcheon, Daniel C.	185
494325	Mar. 28	Curtis, John D.	149
494326	Mar. 28	Curtis, John D.	156–58
494551	Apr. 4	Curtis, John D.	18, 19
496974	May 9	Guilleaume, Theodore	150
501129	July 11	Allis, Thomas V.	321

INDEX TO PATENTEES WITH PATENTS

A

INDEX TO WIRES AND FIGURES

C

D

E

F

G

H

K

L

M

R

S